The Wright Brothers' Engines
And Their Design

Kitty Hawk Flyer with original Wright engine poised on launching rail at Kill Devil Hill, near Kitty Hawk, North Carolina, 24 November 1903, the month before the Wrights achieved man's first powered and controlled flight in a heavier-than-air craft.

Reproduction of the first engine, built by Pratt & Whitney, as displayed in Wright Brothers National Memorial at Kitty Hawk. Engine is mounted in a reproduction of the Wrights' *Flyer* built by the National Capital Section of the Institute of the Aeronautical Sciences (now the American Institute of Aeronautics and Astronautics). Engine and plane were donated in 1963 to the National Park Service Cape Hatteras National Seashore.

SMITHSONIAN ANNALS OF FLIGHT • NUMBER 5

SMITHSONIAN INSTITUTION • NATIONAL AIR AND SPACE MUSEUM

The Wright Brothers' Engines
And Their Design

Leonard S. Hobbs

SMITHSONIAN INSTITUTION PRESS
CITY OF WASHINGTON
1971

Smithsonian Annals of Flight

Numbers 1–4 constitute volume one of *Smithsonian Annals of Flight*. Subsequent numbers will bear no volume designation, which has been dropped. The following earlier numbers of *Smithsonian Annals of Flight* are available from the Superintendent of Documents as indicated below:

1. The First Nonstop Coast-to-Coast Flight and the Historic T–2 Airplane, by Louis S. Casey. 1964. 90 pages, 43 figures, appendix, bibliography. Out of print.
2. The First Airplane Diesel Engine: Packard Model DR–980 of 1928, by Robert B. Meyer. 1964. 48 pages, 37 figures, appendix, bibliography. Price 60¢.
3. The Liberty Engine 1918–1942, by Philip S. Dickey. 1968. 110 pages, 20 figures, appendix, bibliography. Price 75¢.
4. Aircraft Propulsion: A Review of the Evolution of Aircraft Piston Engines, by C. Fayette Taylor. 1971 viii + 134 pages, 72 figures, appendix, bibliography of 601 items. Price $1.75.

For sale by Superintendent of Documents, Government Printing Office
Washington, D.C. 20402 - Price 60 cents

Foreword

In this fifth number of *Smithsonian Annals of Flight* Leonard S. Hobbs analyzes the original Wright *Kitty Hawk Flyer* engine from the point of view of an aeronautical engineer whose long experience in the development of aircraft engines gives him unique insight into the problems confronting these remarkable brothers and the ingenious solutions they achieved. His review of these achievements also includes their later vertical 4- and 6-cylinder models designed and produced between 1903 and 1915.

The career of Leonard S. (Luke) Hobbs spans the years that saw the maturing of the aircraft piston engine and then the transition from reciprocating power to the gas turbine engine. In 1920 he became a test engineer in the Power Plant Laboratory of the Army Air Service at McCook Field in Dayton, Ohio. There, and later as an engineer with the Stromberg Motor Devices Corporation, he specialized in aircraft engine carburetors and developed the basic float-type to the stage of utility where for the first time it provided normal operation during airplane evolutions, including inverted flight.

Joining Pratt & Whitney Aircraft in 1927 as Research Engineer, Hobbs advanced to engineering manager in 1935 and in 1939 took over complete direction of its engineering. He was named vice president for engineering for all of United Aircraft in 1944, and was elected vice chairman of United Aircraft in 1956, serving in that capacity until his retirement in 1958. He remained a member of the board of directors until 1968. Those years saw the final development of Pratt & Whitney's extensive line of aircraft piston engines which were utilized by the United States and foreign air forces in large quantities and were prominent in the establishment of worldwide air transportation.

In 1963 Hobbs was awarded the Collier Trophy for having directed the design and development of the J57 turbojet, the country's first such engine widely used in both military service and air transportation.

He was an early fellow of the Institute of Aeronautical Sciences (later the American Institute of Aeronautics and Astronautics), served for many years on the Powerplant Committee of the National Advisory Committee for Aeronautics, and was the recipient of the Presidential Certificate of Merit.

FRANK A. TAYLOR, *Acting Director*
National Air and Space Museum

March 1970

v

Contents

Acknowledgments

As is probably usual with most notes such as this, however short, before completion the author becomes indebted to so many people that it is not practical to record all the acknowledgments that should be made. This I regret extremely, for I am most appreciative of the assistance of the many who responded to my every request. The mere mention of the Wright name automatically opened almost every door and brought forth complete co-operation. I do not believe that in the history of the country there has been another scientist or engineer as admired and revered as they are.

I must, however, name a few who gave substantially of their time and effort and without whose help this work would not be as complete as it is. Gilmoure N. Cole, A. L. Rockwell, and the late L. Morgan Porter were major contributors, the latter having made the calculations of the shaking forces, the volumetric efficiency, and the connecting rod characteristics of the 1903 engine. Louis P. Christman, who was responsible for the Smith-sonian drawings of this engine and also supervised the reconstruction of the 1905 Wright airplane, supplied much information, including a great deal of the history of the early engines. Opie Chenoweth, one of the early students of the subject, was of much assisstance; and I am indebted to R. V. Kerley for the major part of the data on the Wrights' shop engine.

Also, I must express my great appreciation to the many organizations that cooperated so fully, and to all the people of these organizations and institutions who gave their assistance so freely. These include the following:

Air Force Museum, Wright-Patterson Air Force Base, Ohio
Carillon Park Museum, Dayton, Ohio
Connecticut Aeronautical Historial Association, Hebron, Connecticut
Fredrick C. Crawford Museum, Cleveland, Ohio
Historical Department, Daimler Benz A. G., Stuttgart-Unterturkheim, West Germany
Engineers Club, Dayton, Ohio
Deutsches Museum, Munich, West Germany
Educational and Musical Arts, Inc., Dayton, Ohio
Henry Ford Museum, Dearborn, Michigan
Franklin Institute, Philadelphia, Pennsylvania

Howell Cheney Technical School, Manchester, Connecticut
Library of Congress, Washington, D.C.
Naval Air Systems Command, U. S. Navy, Washington, D.C.
Science Museum, London, England
Victoria and Albert Museum, London, England

In particular, very extensive contributions were made by the Smithsonian
Institution and by the United Aircraft Corporation through its Library,
through the Pratt & Whitney Aircraft Division's entire Engineering Department and its Marketing and Product Support Departments, and through
United Aircraft International.

The Beginnings

The general history of the flight engines used by the Wright Brothers is quite fascinating and fortunately rather well recorded.[1] The individual interested in obtaining a reasonably complete general story quickly is referred to three of the items listed in the short bibliography on page 69. The first, *The Papers of Wilbur and Orville Wright*, is a primary source edited by the authority on the Wright brothers, Marvin W. McFarland of the Library of Congress; a compact appendix to volume 2 of the *Papers* contains most of the essential facts. This source is supplemented by the paper of Baker[2] and the accompanying comments by Chenoweth, presented at the National Aeronautics Meeting of the Society of Automotive Engineers on 17 April 1950. Aside from their excellence as history, these publications are outstanding for the manner in which those responsible demonstrate their competence and complete mastery of the sometimes complex technical part of the Wright story.

The consuming interest of the Wrights, of course, was in flight as such, and in their thinking the required power unit was of only secondary importance. However, regardless of their feeling about it, the unit was an integral part of their objective and, due to the prevailing circumstances, they very early found themselves in the aircraft engine business despite their inexperience. This business was carried on very successfully, against increasingly severe competition, until Orville Wright withdrew from commercial activity and dissolved the Wright Company. The time span covered approximately the twelve years from 1903 to 1915, during the first five years of which they designed and built for their own use several engines of three different experimental and demonstration designs. In the latter part of the period, they manufactured and sold engines commercially, and during this time they marketed three models, one of which was basically their last demonstration design. A special racing engine was also built and flown

---

[1] An extensive bibliography, essentially as complete at this time as when it was compiled in the early 1950s, is given on pages 1240–1242 of volume 2 of *The Papers of Wilbur and Orville Wright*, 1953.

[2] Max P. Baker was a technical adviser to the Wright estate and as such had complete access to all of the material it contained.

during this period. Accurate records are not available but altogether, they produced a total of something probably close to 200 engines of which they themselves took a small number for their various activities, including their school and flying exhibition work which at one time accounted for a very substantial part of their business. A similar lack of information concerning their competition, which expanded rapidly after the Wright's demonstrations, makes any comparisons a difficult task. The Wrights were meticulous about checking the actual performance of their engines but at that time ratings generally were seldom authenticated and even when different engines were tried in the same airplane the results usually were not measured with any accuracy or recorded with any permanency. There is evidence that the competition became effective enough to compel the complete redesign of their engine so that it was essentially a new model.

For their initial experimentation the Wrights regarded gravity as not only their most reliable power source but also the one most economical and readily available, hence their concentration on gliding. They had correctly diagnosed the basic problem of flight to be that of control, the matter of the best wing shapes being inherently a simpler one which they would master by experiment, utilizing at first gravity and later a wind tunnel. Consequently, the acquisition of a powerplant intended for actual flight was considerably deferred.

Nevertheless, they were continuously considering the power requirement and its problems. In his September 1901 lecture to the Western Society of Engineers, Wilbur Wright made two statements: "Men also know how to build engines and screws of sufficient lightness and power to drive these planes at sustaining speed"; and in conjunction with some figures he quoted of the required power and weight: "Such an engine is entirely practicable. Indeed, working motors of one-half this weight per horsepower [9 pounds per horsepower] have been constructed by several different builders." It is quite obvious that with their general knowledge and the experience they had acquired in designing and building a successful shop engine for their own use, they had no cause to doubt their ability to supply a suitable powerplant when the need arose. After the characteristics of the airframe had been settled, and the engine requirements delineated in rather detailed form, they had reached the point of decision on what they termed the motor problem. Only one major element had changed greatly since their previous consideration of the matter; they had arrived at the point where they not only needed a flight engine, they wanted it quickly.

Nothing has been found that would indicate how much consideration they had given to forms of power for propulsion other than the choice they had apparently made quite early—the internal-combustion, four-

2

stroke-cycle piston engine. Undoubtedly, steam was dismissed without being given much, if any, thought. On the face of it, the system was quite impractical for the size and kind of machine they planned; but it had been chosen by Maxim for his experiments,[3] and some thirty-five or forty years later a serious effort to produce an aviation engine utilizing steam was initiated by Lockheed. On the other hand internal-combustion two-stroke-cycle piston engines had been built and used successfully in a limited way. And since, at that time, it was probably not recognized that the maximum quantity of heat it is possible to dissipate imposed an inherent limitation on the power output of the internal-combustion engine, the two-stroke-cycle may have appeared to offer a higher output from a given engine size than the four-stroke-cycle could produce. Certainly, it would have seemed to promise much less torque variation for the same output, something that was of great importance to the Wrights. Against this, the poor scavenging efficiency of the two-stroke operation, and most probably its concurrent poor fuel economy, were always evident; and, moreover, at that time the majority of operating engines were four-stroke-cycle. Whatever their reasoning, they selected for their first powered flight the exact form of prime mover that continued to power the airplane until the advent of the aircraft gas turbine more than forty years later.

The indicated solution to their problem of obtaining the engine—and the engine that would seem by all odds most reliable—would have been to have a unit produced to their specifications by one of the best of the experienced engine builders, and to accomplish this, the most effective method would be to use the equivalent of a bid procedure. This they attempted, and sent out a letter of inquiry to a fairly large number of manufacturers. Although no copy of the letter is available, it is rather well established that it requested the price of an engine of certain limited specifications which would satisfy their flight requirements, but beyond this there is little in the record.

A more thorough examination of the underlying fundamentals, however, discloses many weaknesses in the simple assumptions that made the choice of an experienced builder seem automatic. A maximum requirement limited to only one or two units offered little incentive to a manufacturer already successfully producing in his field, and the disadvantage of the limited quantity was only accentuated by the basic requirement for a technical performance in excess of any standard of the time. Certainly there was no promise of any future quantity business or any other substantial reward. Orville Wright many times stated that they had no desire to produce their own

---

[3] In the 1890s the wealthy inventor Sir Hiram Stevens Maxim conducted an experiment of considerable magnitude with a flying machine that utilized a twin-cylinder compound steam powerplant. It was developed to the flight-test stage.

engine, but it is doubtful that they had any real faith in the buying procedure, for they made no attempt to follow up their first inquiries or to expand the original list.

Whatever the reasoning, their judgment of the situation is obvious; they spent no time awaiting results from the letter but almost immediately started on the task of designing and building the engine themselves. Perhaps the generalities were not as governing as the two specific factors whose immediate importance were determining: cost and time. The Wrights no doubt realized that a specially designed, relatively high performance engine in very limited hand-built quantities would not only be an expensive purchased article but would also take considerable time to build, even under the most favorable circumstances. So the lack of response to their first approach did not have too much to do with their ultimate decision to undertake this task themselves.

The question of the cost of the Wrights' powerplants is most intriguing, as is that of their entire accomplishment. No detailed figures of actual engine costs are in the record, and it is somewhat difficult to imagine just how they managed to conduct an operation requiring so much effort and such material resources, given the income available from their fairly small bicycle business. The only evidence bearing on this is a statement that the maximum income from this business averaged $3,000 a year,[4] which of course had to cover not only the airplane and engine but all personal and other expenses. Yet they always had spare engines and spare parts available; they seemingly had no trouble acquiring needed materials and supplies, both simple and complex; and they apparently never were hindered at any time by lack of cash or credit. The only mention of any concern about money is a statement by Wilbur Wright in a letter of 20 May 1908 when, about to sail for France for the first public demonstrations, he wrote: "This plan would put it to the touch quickly and also help ward off an approaching financial stringency which has worried me very much for several months." It is a remarkable record in the economical use of money, considering all they had done up to that time. The myth that they had been aided by the earnings of their sister Katherine as a school teacher was demolished long ago.

The decision to build the engine themselves added one more requirement, and possibly to some extent a restriction, to the design. They undoubtedly desired to machine as much of the engine as possible in their own shop, and the very limited equipment they had would affect the variety of features and constructions that could be utilized, although experi-

---

[4] Fred C. Kelly, *Miracle at Kitty Hawk*, 1951.

enced machine shops with sophisticated equipment were available in Dayton and it is obvious that the Wrights intended to, and did, utilize these when necessary. The use of their own equipment, of course, guaranteed that the parts they could handle themselves would be more expeditiously produced. They commenced work on the design and construction shortly before Christmas in 1902.

The subject of drawings of the engine is interesting, not only as history but also because it presents several mysteries. Taylor[5] stated, "We didn't make any drawings. One of us would sketch out the part we were talking about on a piece of scrap paper . . ." Obviously somewhere in the operation some dimensions were added, for the design in many places required quite accurate machining. Orville Wright's diary of 1904 has the entry, "Took old engine apart to get measurements for making new engine." Finally, no Wright drawings of the original engine have been seen by anyone connected with the history or with the Wright estate. In the estate were two drawings (now at the Franklin Institute)', on heavy brown wrapping paper, relating to one of the two very similar later engines built in 1904; one is of a cylinder and connecting rod, the other is an end view of the engine. Thus even if the very ingenious drafting board now in the Wright Museum at Carillon Park was available at the time there is no indication that it was used to produce what could properly be called drawings of the first engine.

There are in existence, however, two complete sets of drawings, both of which purport to represent the 1903 flight engine. One set was made in England for the Science Museum in the two years 1928 and 1939. The 1928 drawings were made on receipt of the engine, which was not disassembled, but in 1939 the engine was removed from the airplane, disassembled, the original 1928 drawings were corrected and added to, and the whole was made into one very complete and usable set. The other set was prepared in Dayton, Ohio, for Educational and Musical Arts, Inc.,[6] and was donated to the Smithsonian Institution. This latter set was started under the direction of Orville Wright, who died shorly after the work had been commenced.

---

[5] Charles E. Taylor (Charley Taylor to the many who knew him) was in effect the superintendent of and also the only employee to work in the original small machine shop. A most versatile and efficient mechanic and machine operator, he made many parts for all of the early engines, and in the manner of the experimental machinist, worked mainly from sketches. He also had charge of the bicycle shop and its business in the absence of the Wrights.

[6] This is a charitable agency set up by the late Colonel and Mrs. E. A. Deeds primarily for the purpose of building and supporting the Deeds Carillon and the Carillon Park Museum in Dayton, Ohio.

The two sets of drawings, that is, the one of the Science Museum and that made in Dayton for the Smithsonian Institution, cannot be reconciled in the matter of details. Hardly any single dimension is exactly the same and essentially every part differs in some respect. Many of the forms of construction differ and even the firing order of the two engines is not the same, so that in effect the drawings show two different engines.

The primary trouble is, of course, that the exact engine which flew in 1903 is no longer in existence, and since no original drawings of it exist, there is considerable doubt about its details. The engine had its crankcase broken in an accident to the airframe (this was caused by a strong wind gust immediately following the last of the first series of flights at Kitty Hawk), and when it was brought back to Dayton it was for some inexplicable reason completely laid aside, even though it presumably contained many usable parts. When the engine was disassembled to obtain measurements for constructing the 1904 engines, again apparently no drawings were made. In February 1906 Orville Wright wrote that all the parts of the engine were still in existence except the crankcase; but shortly after

Figure 1.—First flight engine, 1903, valve side.
(Photo courtesy Science Museum, London.)

Figure 2.—First flight engine, 1903, underside and flywheel end. (Photo courtesy Science Museum, London.)

this the crankshaft and flywheel were loaned for exhibition purposes and were never recovered. In 1926 the engine was reassembled for an exhibition and in 1928 it was again reassembled for shipment to England. The only parts of this particular engine whose complete history is definitely known are the crankshaft and flywheel, which were taken from the 1904–1905 flight engine. This latter engine, now in the restored 1905 airplane in the Carillon Park Museum in Dayton, does not contain a crankshaft, and in its place incorporates a length of round bar stock.

In late 1947 work on the Educational and Musical Arts drawings was initiated under the direction of Louis P. Christman and carried through to completion by him. Christman has stated that Orville Wright was critical of the Science Museum drawings but just what he thought incorrect is not known. Whatever his reasons, he did encourage Christman to undertake the major task of duplication. Christman worked directly with Orville Wright for a period of six weeks and had access to all the records and parts the Wrights had preserved. The resultant drawings are also very complete and, regardless of the differences between these two primary sets, both give a sufficiently accurate picture of the first engine for all purposes except that of exact reproduction in every detail.

There exists a still unsolved puzzle in connection with what seems to be yet another set of drawings of the first engine. In December 1943, in writing to the Science Museum telling of his decision to have the airplane and engine brought back to the United States, Orville Wright stated, "I have complete and accurate drawings of the engine. I shall be glad to furnish them if you decide to make a replica." [7] No trace of these particular drawings can be found in any of the museums, institutions, or other repositories that normally should have acquired them and the executors of Orville Wright's estate have no record or knowledge of them. The date of his letter is four years before the Dayton drawings were commenced; and when Christman was working on these with Orville Wright they had copies of the Science Museum drawings, with complete knowledge of their origin, yet Christman has no knowledge of the drawings referred to in Orville's letter to the Museum. Finally, the evidence is quite conclusive that there were no reproducible or permanent drawings made at the time the first engine was constructed, and, of course, the reconstructed engine itself was sent to England in 1928 and not returned to this country until 1948. [8]

---

[7] The Science Museum expressed a desire to have these but never recieved them. There is a reference to them in a letter to the Museum from the executors of his estate dated 20 February 1948, but is seems rather obvious from the text that by this time the drawings mentioned by Orville Wright in his 1943 letter had become confused with those being prepared by Christman for the Smithsonian Institution. The Science Museum did have constructed from its own drawings a very fine replica which is completely operable at this time.

[8] There is a third set of drawings prepared by the Ford Motor Company also marked as being of the 1903 engine and these are rather well distributed in various museums and institutions. What this set is based on has been impossible to determine but it is indicated from the existence of actual engines and parts and the probable date of their preparation (no date is given on the drawings themselves) that they were copied from drawings previously made, and therefore add nothing to them. The Orville Wright-Henry Ford friendship originated rather late, considering Ford's avid interest in history and mechanical things. This tardiness could possibly have been the result of Wright coolness—a coolness caused by a report, at the time the validity of the Wright patents was being so strongly contested, that Ford had advised some of those opposing the Wrights to persevere and to obtain the services of his patent counsel who had been successful in overturning the Selden automobile patent. If this barrier ever existed it was surmounted, and Ford spent much effort and went to considerable expense to collect the Wright home and machine shop for his Dearborn museum. The shop equipment apparently had been widely scattered and its retrieval was a major task. It is most likely that the drawings resulted from someone's effort to follow out an order to produce a set of Ford drawings of the original engine. A small scale model of the 1903 flight engine, constructed under the supervision of Charles Taylor, is contained in the Dearborn Museum.

The Engine of the First Flight, 1903

In commencing the design of the first engine, the first important decision arrived at was that of the number and size of the cylinders to be employed and the form in which they would be combined, although it is unlikely that this presented any serious problem. In a similar situation Manly, when he was working on the engine for the Langley Aerodrome,[9] was somewhat perturbed because he did not have access to the most advanced technical knowledge, since the automobile people who were at that time the leaders in the development of the internal combustion engine, tended for competitive reasons to be rather secretive about their latest advancements and designs. But although the standard textbooks may not have been very helpful to him, there were available such volumes as W. Worby Beaumont's *Motor Vehicles and Motors* which contained in considerable detail descriptions and illustrations of the best of the current automobile engines. The situations of Manly and the Wrights differed, however, in that whereas the Wrights' objective was certainly a technical performance considerably above the existing average, Manly's goal was that of something so far beyond this average as to have been considered by many impossible. Importantly, the Wrights had their own experience with their shop engine and a good basic general knowledge of the size of engine that would be necessary to meet their requirements.

Engine roughness was of primary concern to them. In the 1902 description of the engine they sent to various manufacturers, they had stated: ". . . and the engine would be free from vibration." Even though their requirement for a smooth engine was much more urgent than merely to avoid the effect of roughness on the airplane frame, they were faced, before they made their first powered flight, with the basic problem with which the airplane has had to contend for over three-quarters of its present life span: that is, it was necessary to utilize an explosion engine in a structure which, because of weight limitations, had to be made the lightest and hence frailest that could possibly be devised and yet serve its primary purpose. However

---

[9] Charles L. Manly was engaged in the development of the engine for the Langley Aerodrome. See also footnote to Table on page 62.

great the difficulty may have appeared, in the long view, the fault was certainly a relatively minor one in the overall development of the internal combustion engine—that wonderful invention without which their life work would probably never have been so completely successful while they lived, and which, even aside from its partnership with the airplane, has so profoundly affected the nature of the world in which we live.

It seems quite obvious that to the Wrights vibration, or roughness, was predominantly if not entirely caused by the explosion forces, and they were either not completely aware of the effects of the other vibratory forces or they chose to neglect them. Although crankshaft counterweights had been in use as far back as the middle 1800s, the Wrights never incorporated them in any of their engines; and despite the inherent shaking force in the 4-in-line arrangement, they continued to use it for many years.

The choice of four cylinders was obviously made in order to get, for smoothness, what in that day was "a lot of small cylinders"; and this was sound judgment. Furthermore, although the majority of automobiles at that time had engines with fewer than four cylinders, for those that did the in-line form was standard and well proven, and, in fact, Daimler was then operating engines of this general design at powers several times the minimum the Wrights had determined necessary for their purpose.

What fixed the exact cylinder size, that is, the "square" 4x4-in. form, is not recorded, nor is it obvious by supposition. Baker says it was for high displacement and low weight, but these qualities are also greatly affected by many other factors. The total displacement of just over 200 cu in. was on the generous side, given the horsepower they had determined was necessary, but here again the Wrights were undoubtedly making the conservative allowances afterwards proven habitual, to be justified later by greatly increased power requirements and corresponding outputs. The Mean Effective Pressure (MEP), based on their indicated goal of 8 hp, would be a very modest 36 psi at the speed of 870 rpm at which they first tested the engine, and only 31 psi at the reasonably conservative speed of 1000 rpm. The 4x4-in. dimension would provide a cylinder large enough so that the engine was not penalized in the matter of weight and yet small enough to essentially guarantee its successful operation, as cylinders of considerably larger bore were being utilized in automobiles. That their original choice was an excellent one is rather well supported by the fact that in all the different models and sizes of engines they eventually designed and built, they never found it necessary to go to cylinders very much larger than this.

A second basic determination which was made either concurrently or even possibly in advance of that of the general form and size was in the matter of the type of cylinder cooling to adopt. Based on current practice

Figure 3.—First flight engine, 1903, installed in the Kitty Hawk airplane, as exhibited in the Science Museum. (Photo courtesy the Science Museum, London.)

that had proven practical, there were three possibilities, all of which were in use in automobiles: air, water, or a combination of the two. It is an interesting commentary that Fernand Forest's[10] proposed 32-cylinder aircraft engine of 1888 was to be air-cooled, that Santos-Dumont utilized an air-cooled Clement engine in his dirigible flights of 1903, and that the Wrights had chosen air cooling for their shop engine. With the promise of simplicity and elimination of the radiator, water and piping, it would seem, offhand, that this would be the Wrights' choice for their airplane; but they were probably governed by the fact that not only was the water-cooled type predominant in automobile practice, but that the units giving the best and highest performance in general service were all water cooled. In their subsequent practice they never departed from this original decision, although

---

[10] Fernand Forest, *Les Bateaux Automobiles,* 1906.

Wilbur Wright's notebook of 1904–1907 contains an undated weight estimate by detailed parts for an 8-cylinder air-cooled engine. Unfortunately, the proposed power output is not recorded, so their conception of the relative weight of the air-cooled form is not disclosed.

One of the most important decisions relating to the powerplant—one which was probably made long before they became committed to the design itself—was a determination of the method of transmission of power to the propeller, or propellers. A lingering impression exists that the utilization of a chain drive for this purpose was a natural inheritance from their bicycle background. No doubt this experience greatly simplified the task of adaptation but a merely cursory examination shows that even if they had never had any connection with bicycles, the chain drive was a logical solution, considering every important element of the problem. The vast majority of automobiles of the time were chain driven, and chains and sprockets capable of handling a wide range of power were completely developed and available. Further, at that time they had no accurate knowledge of desirable or limiting propeller and engine speeds. The chain drive offered a very simple and inexpensive method of providing for a completely flexible range of speed ratios. The other two possibilities were both undesirable: the first, a simple direct-driven single propeller connected to the crankshaft, provided essentially no flexibility whatsoever in experimentally varying engine or propeller speed ratios, it added an out-of-balance engine torque force to the problem of airplane control, and, finally, it dictated that the pilot would be in the propeller slipstream or the airflow to it; the second, drive shafts and gearing for dual propellers, would have been very heavy and expensive, and most probably would have required a long-time development, with every experimental change in speed ratios requiring a complete change in gears. Again, their original choice was so correct that it lasted them through essentially all their active flying years.

The very substantial advantages of the chain drive were not, however, obtained at no cost. Torque variations in the engine would tend to cause a whipping action in the chain, so that it was vulnerable to rough running caused by misfiring cylinders and, with the right timing and magnitude of normal regular variations, the action could result in destructive forces in the transmission system. This was the basic reason for the Wrights' great fear of "engine vibration," which confined them to the use of small cylinders and made a fairly heavy flywheel necessary on all their engines. When they were requested to install an Austro-Daimler engine in one of their airplanes, they designed a flexible coupling which was interposed between the engine and the propeller drive and this was considered so successful that it was applied to the flywheel of some engines of their last model, the 6–70, "which had been giving trouble in this regard."[11]

Although flat, angled, and vertical engines had all been operated success-fully, the best and most modern automotive engines of the time were vertical, so their choice of a horizontal position was probably dictated either by considerations of drag or their desire to provide a sizable mounting base for the engine, or both. There is no record of their ever having investigated the matter of the drag of the engine, either alone or in combination with the wing. The merit of a vertical versus a horizontal position of the engine was not analogous to that of the pilot, which they had studied, and where the prone position undoubtedly reduced the resistance.

Having decided on the general makeup of their engine, the next major decision was that of just what form the principal parts should take, the most important of these being the cylinders and crankcase. Even at this fairly early date in the history of the internal combustion engine various successful arrangements and combinations were in existence. Individual cylinder construction was by far the most used, quite probably due to its ease of manufacture and adaptability to change. Since 4-cylinder engines were just coming into general use (a few production engines of this type had been utilized as early as 1898), there were few examples of en-bloc or one-piece construction. The original German Daimler Company undoubt-edly was at this time the leader in the development of high-output internal-combustion engines, and in 1902, as an example of what was possible, had placed in service one that possibly approximated 40 hp, which was an MEP of 70 psi. (Almost without exception, quoted power figures of this period were not demonstrated quantities but were based on a formula, of which the only two factors were displacement and rpm.) The cylinders of this Daimler engine were cast iron, the cylinder barrel, head, and water jacket being cast in one piece. The upper part of the barrel and the cylinder head were jacketed, but, surprisingly, the bottom 60 percent of the barrel had no cooling. The cylinders were cast in pairs and bolted to a two-piece aluminum case split at the line of the crankshaft. Ignition was make-and-break and the inlet valves were mechanically actuated. Displacement was 413 cu in. and the rpm was 1050.

Although a few examples of integral crankcase and water jacket combi-nations were in use, the Wrights were being somewhat radical when they decided to incorporate all four cylinders in the one-piece construction, par-ticularly since they also proposed to include the entire crankcase and not just one part of it. It was undoubtedly the most important decision that they were required to make on all the various construction details, and

---

[11] Grover Loening, letter of 10 April 1963, to the Smithsonian Institution.

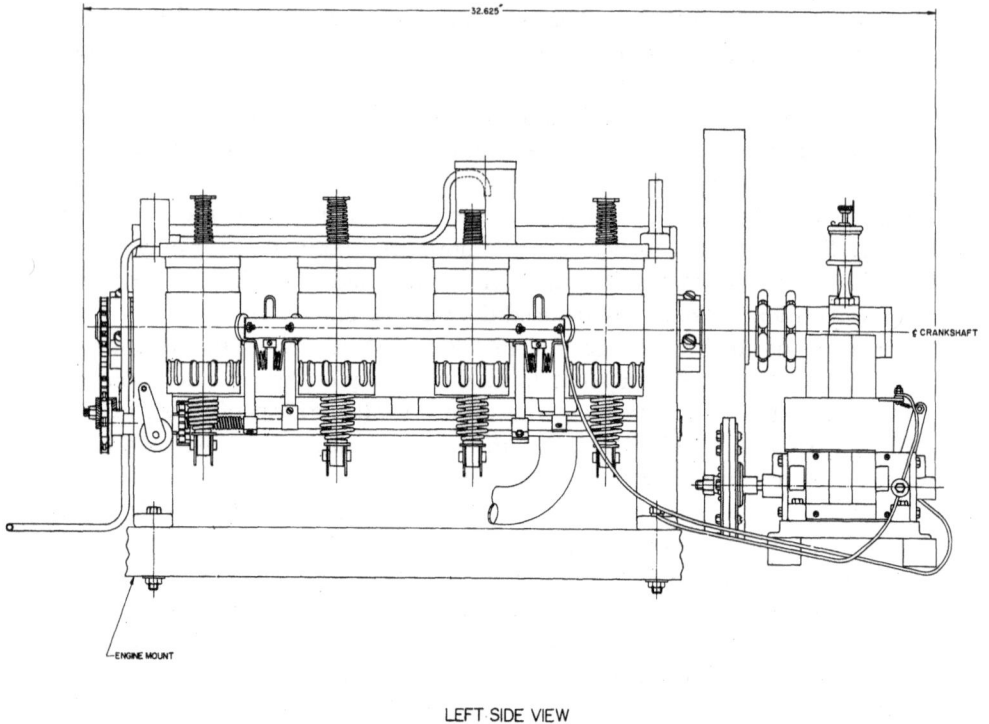

LEFT SIDE VIEW

Figure 4.—First flight engine, 1903, left side and rear views, with
dimensions.   (Drawing courtesy Howell Cheney Technical School.)

probably the one given the most study and investigation. Many factors
were involved, but fundamentally everything went back to their three
basic requirements: suitability, time, and cost. There was no obvious reason
why the construction would not work, and it eliminated a very large number of individual parts and the required time for procuring, machining,
and joining them. Probably one very strong argument was the advanced
state of the casting art, one of the oldest of the mechanical arts in existence
and one the Wrights used in many places, even though other processes were
available. What no doubt weighed heavily was that Dayton had some
first-class foundries. The casting, though intricate and not machinable in
their own shop, could be easily handled in one that was well outfitted.
The pattern was fairly complex but apparently not enough to delay the
project or cause excessive cost.

14

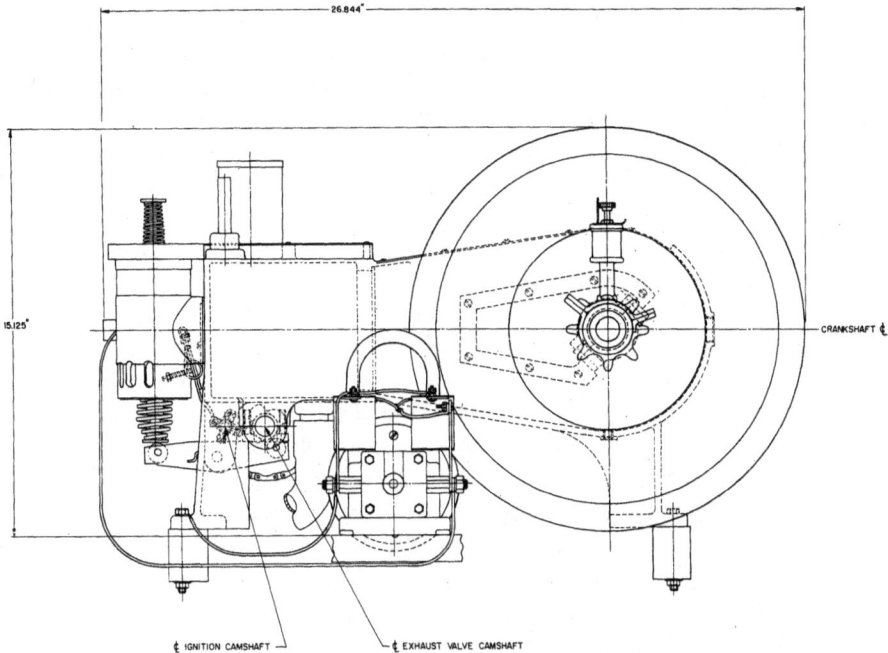

REAR VIEW

DR BY STUDENTS UNDER THE DIRECTION OF JOHN KLEIS	DATE	SCALE	VIEWS — THE WRIGHT BROTHERS AERO ENGINE USED AT KITTY HAWK, N.C. 17 DECEMBER 1903	CK	DATE
	6/1/67		H. CHENEY TECHNICAL SCHOOL, MANCHESTER, CONN.	PWA	6/15/67

The selection of aluminum for the material was an integral part of the basic design decision. Despite the excellence and accuracy of the castings that could be obtained, there was nevertheless a minimum dimension beyond which wall thickness could not be reduced; and the use of either one of the two other proven materials, cast iron or bronze, would have made the body, as they called it, prohibitively heavy. The use of aluminum was not entirely novel at this time, as it had been utilized in many automobile engine parts, particularly crankcases; but its incorporation in this rather uncommon combination represented a bold step. There was no choice in the matter of the alloy to be used, the only proven one available was an 8 percent copper 92 percent aluminum combination.

By means of the proper webs, brackets and bosses, the crankcase would also carry the crankshaft, the rocker arms and bearings, and the intake

15

manifold. The open section of the case at the top was covered with a screw-fastened thin sheet of cold-rolled steel. The main bearing bosses were split at a 45° angle for ease of assembly. The engine support and fastening were provided by four feet, or lugs, cast integral on the bottom corners of the case, and by accompanying bolts (Figure 2). Although the crankcase continued to be pretty much the "body" of the internal combustion aircraft engine throughout its life, the Wrights managed to incorporate in this original part a major portion of the overall engine, and certainly far more than had ever previously been included.

The design of the cylinder barrel presented fairly simple problems involving not much more than those of keeping the sections as thin as possible and devising means of fastening it and of keeping the water jacket tight. They saved considerable weight by making the barrel quite short, so that in operation a large part of the piston extended below the bottom of it; but this could be accepted, as there were no rings below the piston pin (Figure 6). The barrel material, a good grade of cast iron, was an almost automatic choice. In connection with these seemingly predetermined decisions, however, it should be remembered that their goal was an engine which would work without long-time development, and that, with no previous experience in lightweight construction to guide them they were nevertheless compelled to meet a weight limit, so that the thickness of every wall and flange and the length of every thread was important.

With the separate cylinder barrel they were now almost committed to a three-piece cylinder. It would have been possible to combine the barrel and head in a one-piece casting and then devise a method of attachment, but this would have been more complex and certainly heavier. For housing the valves, what was in effect a separate cylindrical, or tubular, box was decided upon. This would lie across the top of the cylinder proper at right angles to the cylinder axis, and the two valves would be carried in the two ends of this box. The cylinder barrel would be brought in at its head end to form a portion of the cylinder head and then extended along its axis in the form of a fairly large boss, a mating boss being provided on one side of the valve box. The cylinder barrel would then be threaded into the valve box and the whole tightened or fastened to the crankcase by means of two sets of threads, one at each end of the barrel proper. This meant that three joints had to be made tight with only two sets of threads. This was accomplished by accurate machining and possibly even hand fitting in combination with a rather thick gasket at the head end, one flat of which bore against two different surfaces. This can be seen in Figure 6, where the circular flange on the valve box contacts both the crankcase and the cylinder barrel. Altogether it was a simple, light, and ingenious solution to a rather complex problem.

16

At this point the question arises: Why was the engine layout such that the exhaust took place close to the operator's ears? It would have been possible, starting with the original design, to turn the engine around so that the exhaust was on the other side. This would have little effect on the location of the center of gravity, and the two main drive chains would then have been of more equal length. However, of the many factors involved, probably one of the principal considerations in arriving at their final decision was the location of the spark-advance control, which was in effect the only control they had of engine output, except for complete shutoff. In their design this was immediately adjacent to the operator; with a turned-around engine, an extension control mechanism of some sort would have been required. The noise of the exhaust apparently became of some concern to them, as Orville's diary in early 1904 contains an entry with a sketch labeled "Design for Muffler for Engine," but there is no further comment.

The problem of keeping joints tight, and for that matter the entire construction itself, were both greatly simplified by their decision to water-jacket only a part of the cylinder head proper, and the valve box not at all. This was undoubtedly the correct decision for their immediate purpose, as again they were effecting savings in time, cost, complexity, and weight. There is nothing in the record, however, to show why they continued this practice long after they had advanced to much greater power outputs and longer flight times. Their own statements show that they were well aware of the effect of the very hot cylinder head on power output and they must also have realized its influence on exhaust-valve temperature.

The cylinder assembly was made somewhat more complicated by their desire to oil the piston and cylinder by means of holes near the crankshaft end in what was, with the engine in the horizontal position, the upper side of the cylinder barrel. This complication was no doubt taken care of by not drilling the holes until a tight assembly had been made by screwing the barrel into place, and by marking the desired location on the barrel. Since this position was determined by a metal-to-metal jam fit of the crankcase and cylinder barrel flange, the barrel would reassemble with the holes in very nearly the same relative position after disassembly.

With the valve box, or housing, cylindrical, the task of locking and fastening the intake and exhaust valve guides and seats in place was easy. The guide was made integral with and in the center of one end of a circular cage, the other end of which contained the valve seat (see Figure 5). Four sections were cut out of the circular wall of the cage so that in effect the seat and guide were joined by four narrow legs, the spaces between which provided passages for the flow of the cylinder gases. These cages were then dropped into the ends of the valve boxes until they came up

17

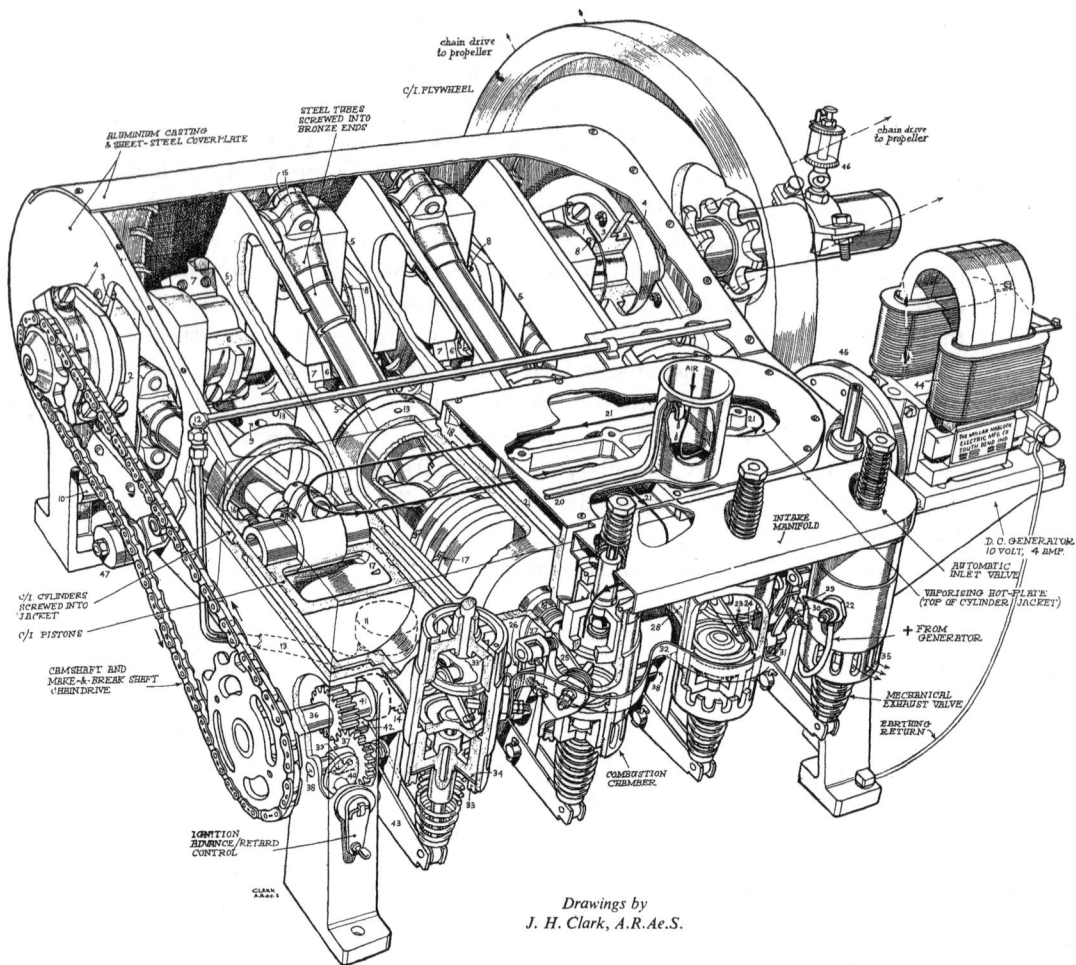

Figure 5.—First flight engine, 1903, assembly. (Phantom cutaway by
J. H. Clark, with key, courtesy *Aeroplane.*)

against machined shoulders and were held in place by internal ring nuts
screwed into the valve box. The intake manifold or passage was placed over
the intake valves so that the intake charge flowed directly into and through
the valve cage around the open valve and into the cylinder. The exhaust
gas, after flowing through the passages in the valve cage, was discharged
directly to the atmosphere through a series of holes machined in one side
of the valve box.

The intake and exhaust valves were identical and of two-piece construction, with the stems screwed tightly into and through the heads and the
protruding ends then peened over. This construction was not novel, having
had much usage behind it, and it continued for a long time in both automobile and aircraft practice. One-piece cast and forged valves were avail-

KEY

1 and 2. Bearing caps in one piece with plate 3.

3. Plated screwed over hole 4 in crank-case end.

4. Key-shaped hole as hole 5 in inter-mediate ribs.

6. Inter-bearings cap (white-metal lined) and screwed to inter-rib halves 7.

8. Splash-drip feed to bearings.

9. Return to pump from each compart-ment of crankcase base ("sump") via gallery 10 and pipe to pump 11 under-neath jacket.

12. Oil feed from pump via rubber tube 13.

13. Drip feeds to cylinders and pistons.

14. Gear drive to pump.

15. Big-end nuts, lock-strip, and shims.

16. Gudgeon-pin lock.

17. Piston-ring retainer pegs.

18. Cylinder liner screwing into jacket.

19. Open-ended "can" admits air.

20. Fuel supply.

21. (Hot) side of water jacket makes sur-face carburetter.

22. Sparking plug (comprising positive electrode 23 and spark-producing make-and-break 24).

25. Lever attached to lever 26 via bearing 27 screwed into chamber neck 28.

26. Levers with mainspring 29 and inter-spring 30, and rocked by "cam" 31.

31. Cam with another alongside (for ad-jacent cylinder).

32. Positive busbar feed to all four cylin-ders.

33. Assembly retaining-rings.

34. Sealing disc.

35. Exhaust outlet ports.

36. Camshaft right along on underside of jacket and also driving oil pump 11 via 14.

37. Spring-loaded sliding pinion drives make-and-break shaft 38 through peg in inclined slot 39.

40. Cam to push pinion 37 along and so alter its angular relation with shaft 38 (to vary timing).

41. Exhaust-valve cams bear on rollers 42 mounted in end of rocker-arms 43.

44. Generator floating coils.

45. Friction-drive off flywheel.

46. Sight-feed lubricator (on stationary sleeve).

47. Hardwood chain tensioner.

able but here again it was a choice of the quick, cheap, and proven answer.

The entire valve system, including guides and seats, was of cast iron, a favorite material of the Wrights, except for the valve stems, which were, at different times, of various carbon steels. Ordinary cold-rolled apparently was used in those of the original engine, but in later engines this was changed to a high-carbon steel.

The piston design presented no difficulty. In some measure this was due to the remarkable similarity that seems to have existed among all the dif-ferent engines of the time in the construction of this particular part, for, although there were some major variations, it was, in fact, almost as if some standard had been adopted. Pistons all were of cast iron and comparatively quite long (it was a number of years before they evolved into the short ones of modern practice); they were almost invariably equipped with three wide piston rings between the piston pin and the head; and, although there were in existence a few pistons with four rings, no oil wiper or other ring seems to have been placed below the piston pin. The Wrights' piston was typical of the time, with the rings pinned in the grooves to prevent turning and the piston pin locked in the piston with a setscrew. In designing this first engine they were, however, apparently somewhat unsure about this latter feature, as they provided the rod with a split little end and a clamping bolt (see Figure 6), so that the pin could be held in the rod if desired; but no examples of this use have been encountered.

The Wrights' selection of an "automatic" or suction-operated inlet valve was entirely logical. Mechanically operated inlet valves were in use and their history went back many years, but the great majority of the engines of that time still had the automatic type, and with this construction one complete set of valve-operating mechanisms was eliminated. They were well aware of the loss of volumetric efficiency inherent in this valve, and apparently went to some pains to obtain from it the best performance possible. Speaking of the first engine, Orville Wright wrote, "Since putting in heavier springs to actuate the valves on our engine we have increased its power to nearly 16 hp and at the same time reduced the amount of gasoline consumed per hour to about one-half of what it was."[12]

Why they continued with this form on their later engines is a question a little more difficult to answer, as they were then seeking more and more power and were building larger engines. The advantages of simplicity and a reduced number of parts still existed, but there also was a sizable power increase to be had which possibly would have more than balanced off the increased cost and weight. They did not utilize mechanical operation until after a major redesign of their last engine model. Very possibly the answer lies in the phenomenon of fuel detonation. This was only beginning to be understood in the late 1920s, and it is quite evident from their writings that they had little knowledge of what made a good fuel in this respect. It is fairly certain, however, that they did know of the existence of cylinder "knock," or detonation, and particularly that the compression ratio had a major effect on it. The ratios they utilized on their different engines varied considerably, ranging from what, for that time, was medium to what was relatively high. The original flight engine had a compression ratio of 4.4:1. The last of their service engines had a compression ratio about twenty percent under that of the previous series—a clear indication that they considered that they had previously gone too high. Quite possibly they con-

---

[12]Assuming a rich mixture, consumption of all the air, and an airbrake thermal efficiency of 24.50% for the original engine, the approximate volumetric efficiency of the cylinder is calculated to have been just under 40%.

cluded that increasing the amount of the cylinder charge seemed to bring on detonation, and that the complication of the mechanical inlet valve was therefore not warranted.

The camshaft for the exhaust valves (101, Figure 6), was chain driven from the crankshaft and was carried along the bottom of the crankcase in three babbit-lined bearings in bearing boxes or lugs cast integral with the case. Both the driving chain and the sprockets were standard bicycle parts, and a number of bicycle thread standards and other items of bicycle practice were incorporated in several places in the engine, easing their construction task. The shaft itself, of mild carbon steel, was hollow and on each side of an end bearing sweated-on washers provided shoulders to locate it longitudinally. Its location adjacent to the valves, with the cam operating directly on the rocker arm, eliminated push rods and attendant parts, a

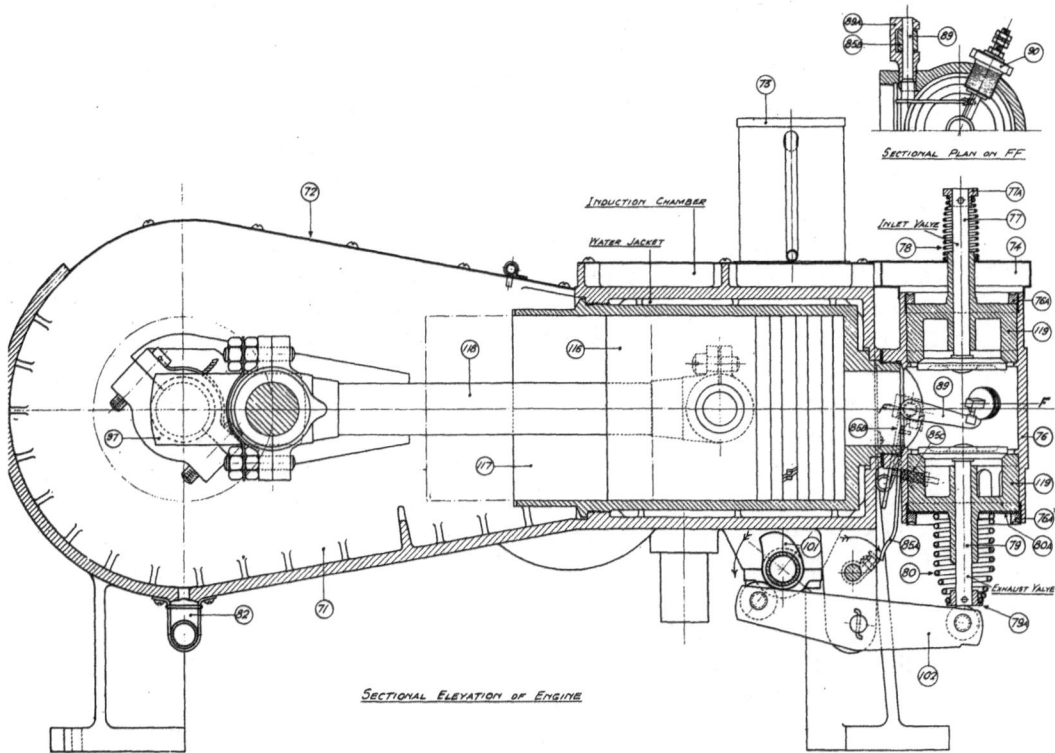

Figure 6.—First flight engine, 1903, cross section.
(Drawing courtesy Science Museum, London.)

21

major economy. The cams were machined as separate parts and then sweated onto the shaft. Their shape shows the principal concern in the design to have been obtaining maximum valve capacity—that is, a quite rapid opening with a long dwell. This apparent desire to get rid of the exhaust gas quickly is manifested again in the alacrity with which they adopted a piston-controlled exhaust port immediately they had really mastered flight and were contemplating more powerful and more durable engines. This maximum-capacity theory of valve operation, with its neglect of acceleration forces and seating velocities, may well have been at least partially if not largely the cause of their exhaust-valve troubles and the seemingly disproportionate amount of development they devoted to this part, as reported by Chenoweth, although it is also true that the exhaust valve continued to present a problem in the aircraft piston engine for a great many years after, even with the most scientific of cam designs.

The rocker arm (102, Figure 6) is probably the best example of a small part which met all of their many specific requirements with an extreme of simplicity. It consisted of two identical side pieces, or walls, of sheet steel shaped to the desired side contour of the assembly, in which were drilled three holes, one in each end, to carry the roller axles, and the third in the approximate middle for the rocker axle shaft proper. This consisted of a piece of solid rod positioned by cotter pins in each end outside the side walls (see Figure 5). The assembly was made by riveting over the ends of the roller axles so that the walls were held tightly against the shoulders on the axles, thus providing the correct clearance for the rollers. The construction was so light and serviceable that it was essentially carried over to the last engine the Wrights ever built.

The basic intake manifold (see Figure 5) consisted of a very low flat box of sheet steel which ran across the tops of the valve boxes and was directly connected to the top of each of them so that the cages, and thus the valves, were open to the interior of the manifold. Through an opening in the side toward the engine the manifold was connected to a flat induction chamber (21, Figure 5) which served to vaporize the fuel and mix it with the incoming air. This chamber was formed by screw-fastening a piece of sheet steel to vertical ribs cast integral with the crankcase, the crankcase wall itself thus forming the bottom of the chamber. A beaded sheet-steel cylinder resembling a can (73, Figure 6) but open at both ends was fastened upright to the top of this chamber. In the absence of anything else, this can could be called the carburetor, as a fuel supply line entered the cylinder near the top and discharged the fuel into the incoming air stream, both the fuel and air then going directly into the mixing chamber. The can was attached near one corner of the chamber, and vertical baffles, also cast integral with the case, were so located that the incoming mixture was

Figure 7.—First flight engine, 1903: cylinder, valve box, and gear mechanism; below, miscellaneous parts. (Photos courtesy Science Museum, London, and Louis P. Christman.)

forced to circulate over the entire area of exposed crankcase inside the chamber before it reached the outlet to the manifold proper, the hot surface vaporizing that part of the fuel still liquid.

Fuel was gravity fed to the can through copper and rubber tubing from a tank fastened to a strut, several feet above the engine. Of the two valves placed in the fuel line, one was a simple on-off shutoff cock and the other a type whose opening could be regulated. The latter was adjusted to supply the correct amount of fuel under the desired flight operating condition; the shutoff cock was used for starting and stopping. The rate of fuel supply to the engine would decrease as the level in the fuel tank dropped, but as the head being utilized was a matter of several feet and the height of the supply tank a matter of inches, the fuel-air ratio was still maintained well within the range that would ignite and burn properly in the contemplated one-power condition of their flight operation.

This arrangement is one of the best of the many illustrations of how by the use of foresight and ingenuity the Wrights met the challenge of a complex requirement with a simple device, for while carburetors were not in the perfected stage later attained, quite good ones that would both control power output and supply a fairly constant fuel-air mixture over a range of operating conditions were available, but they were complex, heavy, and expensive. The arrangement, moreover, secured at no cost a good vaporizer, or modern "hot spot." In their subsequent engines they took the control of the fuel metering away from the regulating valve and gravity tank combination and substituted an engine-driven fuel pump which provided a fuel supply bearing a fairly close relationship to engine speed.

The reasons behind selection of the type of ignition used, and the considerations entering into the decision, are open to speculation, as are those concerning many other elements that eventually made up the engine. Both the high-tension spark plug and low-tension make-and-break systems had been in wide use for many years, with the latter constituting the majority in 1902. Both were serviceable and therefore acceptable, and both required a "magneto." The art of the spark plug was in a sense esoteric (to a certain extent it so remains to this day), but the spark-plug system did involve a much simpler combination of parts: in addition to the plug and magneto there would be needed only a timer, or distributor, together with coils and points, or some substitute arrangement. The make-and-break system, on the other hand, required for each cylinder what was physically the equivalent of a spark plug, that is, a moving arm and contact point inside the cylinder, a spring-loaded snap mechanism to break the contact outside the cylinder, and a camshaft and cams to actuate the breaker mechanism at the proper time. Futhermore, as the Wrights applied it, the system required dry cells and a coil for starting, although these did not accompany the engine in flight. And finally there was the problem of keeping tight the joint where the oscillating shaft required to operate the moving point in the spark plug entered the cylinder.

This is one of the few occasions, if not the only one, when the Wrights chose the more complex solution in connection with a major part—in this particular case, one with far more bits and pieces. However, it did carry with it some quite major advantages. The common spark plug, always subject to fouling or failure to function because of a decreased gap, was not very reliable over a lengthy period, and was undoubtedly much more so in those days when control of the amount of oil inside the cylinder was not at all exact. Make-and-break points, on the other hand, were unaffected by excess oil in the cylinder. Because of this resistance to fouling, the system was particularly suitable for use with the compression-release method of power control which they later utilized, although they probably could not have been looking that far ahead at the time they chose it. High-tension current has always, and rightfully so, been thought of as a troublemaker in service; in Beaumont's 1900 edition of *Motor Vehicles and Motors,* which seems to have been technically the best volume of its time, the editor predicted that low-tension make-and-break ignition would ultimately supersede all other methods. And finally, the large number of small parts required for the make-and-break system could all be made in the Wright Brothers' shop or easily procured, and in the end this was probably the factor, plus reliability, that determined the decision which, all things considered, was the correct one.

There was nothing exceptional about the exact form the Wrights devised. It displayed the usual refined simplicity (the cams were made of a single small piece of strip steel bent to shape and clamped to the ignition camshaft with a simple self-locking screw), and lightness. The ignition camshaft (38, Figure 5), a piece of small-diameter bar stock, was located on the same side as the exhaust valve camshaft, approximately midway between it and the valve boxes, and was operated by the exhaust camshaft through spur gearing. That the Wrights were thinking of something beyond mere hops or short flights is shown by the fact that the ignition points were platinum-faced, whereas even soft iron would have been satisfactory for the duration of all their flying for many years.

The control of the spark timing was effected by advancing or retarding the ignition camshaft in relation to the exhaust valve camshaft. The spur gear (37, Figure 5) driving the ignition camshaft had its hub on one side extended out to provide what was in effect a sleeve around the camshaft integral with the gear. The gear and integral sleeve were slideable on the shaft and the sleeve at one place (39, Figure 5) was completely slotted through to the shaft at an angle of 45° to the longitudinal axis of the shaft. The shaft was driven by a pin tightly fitted in it and extending into the slot. The fore-and-aft position of the sleeve on the shaft was determined by a lever-operated cam (40, Figure 5) on one side and a spring on the other. The movement of the sleeve along the shaft would cause the shaft to rotate in relation to it because of the angle of the slot, thus providing the desired variation in timing of the spark. The "magneto" was a purchased item driven by means of a friction wheel contacting the flywheel, and several different makes were used later, but the original is indicated to have been a Miller-Knoblock (see Figure 5).

The connecting rod is another example of how, seemingly without trouble, they were able to meet the basic requirements they had set for themselves. It consisted of a piece of seamless steel tubing with each end fastened into a phosphor-bronze casting, these castings comprising the big and little ends, drilled through to make the bearings (See Figures 5 and 6). It was strong, stiff and light.[13] Forged rods were in rather wide use at the time and at least one existing engine even had a forged I-beam section design that was tapered down from big to little end. The Wrights' rod was obtained in little more time than it took to make the simple patterns for the two ends. The weight was easily controlled, no bearing liners were necessary, and a very minimum of machining was required. Concerning the big-end material, there exists a contradiction in the records: Baker, whose data are generally most accurate, states that these were babbited, but this must be in error, as the existing engine has straight bronze castings without babbiting, and there is no record, or drawing, or other indication of the bearings having been otherwise.

Different methods of assembling the rod were used. At one time the tube ends were screwed into the bronze castings and pinned, and at another the ends were pinned and soldered. There is an indication that at one time soldering and threads were used in combination. One of the many conflicts between the two primary sets of drawings exists at this point. The Smithsonian drawings show the use at each end of adapters between the rod and end castings, the adapters being first screwed into the castings and pinned and then brazed to the inside of the tube. The Science Museum drawings show the tube section threaded and screwed into the castings. The direct screw assembly method called for accurate machining and hand fitting in order to make the ends of the tubing jam against the bottom of the threaded holes in the castings, and at the same time have the end bearings properly lined up. The weakness of the basic design patently lies

---

[13]A rather thorough stress analysis of the rod shows it to compare very favorably with modern practice. In the absence of an indicator card for the 1903 engine, if a maximum gas pressure of five times the MEP is assumed, the yield-tension factor of safety is measurably higher than that of two designs of piston engines still in wide service, and the column factor of safety only slightly less. The shear stresses in the brazed and threaded joints are so low as to be negligible.

in the joints. It is an attempt to utilize what was probably in the beginning a combination five-piece assembly and later three, in a very highly stressed part where the load was reversing. It gave them considerable trouble from time to time, particularly in the 4-cylinder vertical engines, and was abandoned for a forged I-beam section type in their last engine model; but it was nevertheless the ideal solution for their first engine.

The crankshaft was made from a solid block of relatively high carbon steel which, aside from its bulk and the major amount of machining required, presented no special problems. It was heat-treated to a machinable hardness before being worked on, but was not further tempered. The design was an orthodox straight pin and cheek combination and, as previously noted, there were no counterweights to complicate the machining or assembly. A sizable bearing was provided on each side of each crank of the shaft, which helped reduce the stiffness requirement.

Their only serious design consideration was to maintain the desired strength and still keep within weight limitations. A fundamental that every professional designer knows is that it is with this particular sort of part that weight gets out of control; even an additional 1/16 in., if added in a few places, can balloon the weight. With their usual foresight and planning, the Wrights carefully checked and recorded the weight of each part as it was finished, but even this does not quite explain how these two individuals, inexperienced in multicylinder engines—much less in extra-light construction—could, in two months, bring through an engine which was both operable and somewhat lighter than their specification.

In one matter it would seem that they were quite fortunate. The records are not complete, but with one exception there is no indication of any chronic or even occasional crankshaft failure. This would seem to show that it apparently never happened that any of their designs came out such that the frequency of a vibrating force of any magnitude occurred at the natural frequency of the shaft. Much later, when this type of vibration became understood, it was found virtually impossible, with power outputs of any magnitude, to design an undampened shaft, within the space and weight limitations existing in an ordinary engine, strong enough to withstand the stress generated when the frequency of the imposed vibration approximated the natural frequency of the shaft. The vibratory forces were mostly relatively small in their engines, so that forced vibration probably was not encountered, and the operating speed range of the engines was so limited that the natural frequency always fell outside this range.

The flywheel was about the least complex of any of their engine parts and required little studied consideration, although they did have to balance its weight against the magnitude of the explosion forces which would reach the power transmission chains, with their complete lack of rigidity, a problem about which they were particularly concerned. The flywheel was made of cast iron and was both keyed to and shrunk on the shaft.

Some doubt still exists about the exact method of lubricating the first engine. The unit presently in the airplane has a gear-type oil pump driven by the crankshaft through a worm gear and cross shaft, and the Appendix to the *Papers* states that it was lubricated by a small pump; nevertheless Baker says, after careful research, that despite this evidence, it was not. Also, the drawings prepared by Christman (they were commenced under the supervision of Orville Wright) do not show the oil pump. In March 1905 Wilbur Wright wrote to Chanute, "However we have added oiling and feeding devices to the engine . . ."; but this could possibly have referred to something other than an oil pump. But even if a pump was not included originally, its presence in the present engine is easily explained. Breakage of the crankcase casting caused the retirement of this engine, which was not rebuilt until much later, and the pattern for this part had no doubt long since been altered to incorporate a pump. It was therefore easier in rebuilding to include than to omit the pump, even though this required the addition of a cross shaft and worm gear combination. On later engines, when the pump was used, oil was carried to a small pipe, running along the inside of the case, which had four small drill holes so located as to throw the oil in a jet on the higher, thrust-loaded side of each cylinder. The rods had a sharp scupper on the outside of the big end so placed as also to throw the oil on this same thrust face. Some scuppers were drilled through to carry oil to the rod bearing and some were not.

The first engine was finished and assembled in February 1903 and given its first operating test on 22 February. The Wrights were quite pleased with its operation, and particularly with its smoothness. Their father, Bishop Wright, was the recorder of their satisfaction over its initial performance, but what he noted was probably the afterglow of the ineffable feeling of deep satisfaction that is the reward that comes to every maker of a new engine when it first comes to life and then throbs. They obtained 13 hp originally: later figures went as high as almost 16, but as different engine speeds were utilized it is rather difficult to settle on any single power figure. The most realistic is probably that given in the *Papers* as having been attained later, after an accurate check had been made of the power required to turn a set of propellers at a given rpm. This came out at approximately 12 hp, the design goal having been 8. Following exactly the procedure that exists to this day, the engine went through an extended development period, and it was the end of September 1903 before it was taken, with the airplane, to Kitty Hawk where the historic flights, which have had such a profound effect on the lives of all men, were made on 17 December 1903.

The Engines With Which They Mastered
The Art of Flying

Two more engines of this first general design were built but they differed somewhat from each other as well as from the original. Together with a third 8-cylinder engine these were begun right after the first of the year in 1904, shortly after the Wrights' return from Kitty Hawk. In planning the 8-cylinder engine they were again only being forehanded, but considerably so, in providing more power for increased airplane performance beyond that which might possibly be obtained from the 4-cylinder units. Progress with the 4-cylinder engines was such that they fairly quickly concluded that the 8-cylinder size would not be necessary, and it was abandoned before completion. Exactly how far it was carried is not known. The record contains only a single note covering the final scrapping of the parts that had been completed; and apparently there were no drawings, so that even its intended appearance is not known with any exactness. It was probably a 90° V-type using their original basic cylinder construction.

The changes carried through in the two 4-cylinder engines were not major. The water-cooled area of the cylinder barrel was increased by nearly ten percent but the head remained only partially cooled. In hindsight, this consistent avoidance of complete cylinder-head cooling presents the one most inexplicable of the more important design decisions they made, as it does not appear logical. In the original engine, where the factors of time and simplicity were of paramount importance, this made sense, but now they were contemplating considerably increased power requirements, knowing the effect of temperature on both the cylinder and the weight of cylinder charge, and knowing that valve failure was one of their most troublesome service problems. Nor does it seem that they could have been avoiding complete cylinder cooling through fear of the slightly increased complexity or the difficulty of keeping the water connections and joints tight, for they had faced a much more severe problem in their first engine, where their basic design required that three joints be kept tight with only two sets of threads, and had rather easily mastered it; so there must have been some much more major but not easily discernible factor

29

which governed, for they still continued to use the poorly cooled head, even carrying it over to their next engine series. Very probably they did not know the effect on detonation of a high-temperature fuel-charge.

One of the new engines was intended for use in their future experimental flying and has become known as *No. 2*. It had a bore of $4\frac{1}{8}$ in., incorporated an oil pump, and at some time shortly after its construction a fuel pump was added. The fuel pump was undoubtedly intended to provide a metering system responsive to engine speed and possibly also to eliminate the small inherent variation in flow of the original gravity system.

This engine incorporated a cylinder compression release device not on the original. The exact reason or reasons for the application of the compression release have not been determined, although the record shows it to have been utilized for several different purposes under different operating conditions. Whatever the motivation for its initial application, it was apparently useful, as it was retained in one form or another in subsequent engine models up to the last 6-cylinder design. Essentially it was a manually controlled mechanism whereby all the exhaust valves could be held open as long as desired, thus preventing any normal charge intake or compression in the cylinder. Its one certain and common use was to facilitate starting, the open exhaust valves easing the task of turning the engine over by hand and making priming easy. In flight, its operation had the effect of completely shutting off the power. The propellers would then "windmill" and keep the engine revolving. One advantage stated for this method of operation was that when power was required and the control released, the engine would be at fairly high speed, so that full power was delivered immediately fuel reached the engine. It is also reported to have been used both in making normal landings and in emergencies, when an instant power shutdown was desired. Although it is not clear whether the fuel shutoff cock was intended to be manipulated when the compression release was used for any of these reasons, over the many years of its availability, undoubtedly at one time or another every conceivable combination of operating conditions of the various elements was tried. Because of the pumping power required with at least one valve open during every stroke, the windmilling speed of the engine was probably less than with any other method of completely stopping power output, but whether this difference was large enough to be noticeable, or was even considered, is doubtful.

Since a simple ignition switch was all that was required to stop the power output, regardless of whether a fuel-control valve or a spark-advance control was used, it must be concluded that the primary function of the compression release was to facilitate starting, and any other useful result was something obtained at no cost. The compression release was later generally abandoned, and until the advent of the mechanical starter during the

1920s, starting an engine by "pulling the propeller through" could be a difficult task. With the Wrights' demonstrated belief that frugality was a first principle of design, it is hardly conceivable that they would have accepted for any other reason the complication of the compression-release mechanism if a simple ignition switch would have sufficed.

The compression-release mechanism was kept relatively simple, considering what it was required to accomplish. A small non-revolving shaft was located directly under the rocker arm rollers that actuated the exhaust valves. Four slidable stops were placed on this shaft, each in the proper location, so that at one extreme of their travel they would be directly underneath the rocker roller and at the other extreme completely in the clear. They were positioned along the shaft by a spring forcing them in one direction against a shoulder integral with the shaft, and the shaft was slidable in its bearings, its position being determined by a manually controlled lever. When the lever was moved in one direction the spring pressure then imposed on the stops would cause each of them to move under the corresponding rocker roller as the exhaust valve opened, thus holding the exhaust valve in the open position. When the shaft was moved in the other direction the collar on the shaft would mechanically move the stop from underneath the roller, allowing the valve to return to normal operation.

If the 1903 engine is the most significant of all that the Wrights built and

Figure 8.—Development engine No. 3, 1904–1906, showing auxiliary exhaust port, separate one-piece water-jacket block. (Photo by author.)

flew, then certainly the *No. 2* unit was the most useful, for it was their sole power source during all their flying of 1904 and 1905 and, as they affirmed, it was during this period that they perfected the art, progressing from a short straightaway flight of 59 seconds to a flight controllable in all directions with the duration limited only by the fuel supply. It is to be greatly regretted that no complete log or record was kept of this engine.

The Wrights again exhibited their engineering mastery of a novel basic situation when, starting out to make flight a practical thing, they provided engine *No. 3* to be used for experimental purposes. In so doing they initiated a system which continues to be fundamental in the art of providing serviceable aircraft engines to this day—one that is expensive and time consuming, but for which no substitute has yet been found. Their two objectives were: improvement in performance and improvement in reliability, and the engine was operated rather continuously from early 1904 until well into 1906. Unfortunately, again, no complete record exists of the many changes made and the ideas tested, although occasional notes are scattered through the diaries and notebooks.

In its present form—it is on exhibition at the Engineers Club in Dayton, Ohio—the *No. 3* engine embodies one feature which became standard construction on all the Wright 4-cylinder models. This was the addition of a number of holes in a line part way around the circumference of the cylinder barrel so that they were uncovered by the piston at the end of its stroke toward the shaft, thus becoming exhaust ports (see Figure 9). This arrangement, although not entirely novel, was just beginning to come into use, and in its original form the ports exhausted into a separate chamber, which in turn was evacuated by means of a mechanically operated valve, so that two exhaust valves were needed per cylinder. Elimination of this chamber and the valve arrangement is typical of the Wrights' simplifying procedure, and it would seem that they were among the very first to use this form.[14]

The primary purpose of the scheme was to reduce, by this early release and consequent pressure and temperature drop, the temperature of the exhaust gases passing the exhaust valve, this valve being one of their main sources of mechanical trouble. It is probable that with the automatic intake valves being used there was also a slight effect in the direction of increasing the inlet charge, although with the small area of the ports and the short time of opening, the amount of this was certainly minor. With the original one-piece crankcase and cylinder jacket construction, the incorporation of this auxiliary porting was not easy, but this difficulty was overcome in the development engine by making different castings for the

---

[14]Rankin Kennedy, *Flying Machines—Practice and Design,* 1909.

crankcase itself and for the cylinder jacket and separating them by several inches, so that room was provided between the two for the ports.

This engine demonstrated the most power of any of the flat 4s, eventually reaching an output of approximately 25 hp, which was even somewhat more than that developed by the slightly larger 4⅛-in.-bore flight engine, with which 21 hp was not exceeded. Indicative of the development that had taken place, the performance of the *No. 3* engine was twice the utilized output of the original engine of the same size, an increase that was accomplished in a period of less than three years.

The Wrights were only twice charged with having plagiarized others' work, a somewhat unusual record in view of their successes, and both times apparently entirely without foundation. A statement was published that the 1903 flight engine was a reworked Pope Toledo automobile unit, and it was repeated in an English lecture on the Wright brothers. This was adequately refuted by McFarland but additionally, it must be noted, there was no Pope Toledo company or car when the Wright engine was built. This company, an outgrowth of another which had previously manufactured one- and two-cylinder automobiles, was formed, or reformed, and a Pope license arrangement entered into during the year 1903.

The other incident was connected with Whitehead's activities and designs. Whitehead was an early experimenter in flying, about the time of the Wrights, whose rather extraordinary claims of successful flight were published in the 1901–1903 period but received little attention until very much later. His first engines were designed by a clever engineer, Anton Pruckner, who left at the end of 1901, after which Whitehead himself became solely responsible for them. It was stated that the Wrights visited the Whitehead plant in Bridgeport, Connecticut, and that Wilbur remained for several days, spending his time in their machine shop. This was not only categorically denied by Orville Wright when he heard of it but it is quite obvious that the 1903 or any other of the Wright engine designs bears little resemblance to Pruckner's work. In fact, its principal design features are just the opposite of Pruckner's, who utilized vertical cylinders, the 2-stroke cycle, and air-cooling, which Whitehead at some point changed to water-cooling.[15]

---

[15] Considerable doubt surrounds Whitehead's actual flight accomplishments, but Pruckner's engines were certainly used, as several were sold to early pioneers, including Charles Wittemann. It is probable that the specific power output was not very great, for the air-cooled art of this time was not very advanced and Pruckner had a rather poor fin design. But the change to water cooling eliminated this trouble, and the engines were most simple, should have been relatively quite light, and with enough development could probably have been made into sufficiently satisfactory flying units for that period.

The Four-Cylinder Vertical Demonstration Engine and the First Production Engine

In 1906, while still doing general development work on the flat experimental engine, the Wrights started two new engines, and for the first time the brothers engaged in separate efforts. One was "a modification of the old ones" by Wilbur and the other, "an entirely new pattern" by Orville. There is no record of any of the features of Wilbur's project or what was done in connection with it. Two months after the experimental operation of the two designs began, an entry in Wilbur's diary gives some weight and performance figures for the "4″ x 4″ rebuilt horizontal," and since Orville's design was vertical the data clearly refer to Wilbur's; but since the output is given only in test-fan rpm it does not serve to indicate what had been accomplished and there is no further mention of it.

Orville's design became the most used of any model they produced. It saw them through the years from 1906 to 1911 or 1912, which included the crucial European and United States Army demonstrations, and more engines of this model were manufactured than any of their others including their later 6-cylinder. Although its ancestry is traceable to the original 1903 engine, the design form, particularly the external configuration, was considerably altered. Along with many individual parts it retained the basic conception of four medium-size cylinders positioned in line and driving the propellers through two sprocket wheels. From the general tenor of the record it would seem, despite there being no specific indication, that from this time on Orville served as the leader in engine design, although this occurred with no effect whatsoever on their finely balanced, exactly equal partnership which endured until Wilbur's death in 1912.

The first major change from the 1903 design, putting the engine in an upright instead of flat position, was probably done primarily to provide for a minimum variation in the location of the center of gravity with and without a passenger. Whether or not it had any influence, the vertical cylinder arrangement was becoming predominant in automobile power-plants by this time, and the Wright engines now began to resemble this prevailing form of the internal combustion engine—a basic form that, in a wide variety of uses, was to endure for a long time.

Over the years, the Wrights seem to have made many changes in the engine: the bore was varied at different times, rod assembly methods were altered, and rod ends were changed from bronze to steel. Chenoweth states that on later engines an oil-control ring was added on the bottom of the piston, necessitating a considerable increase in the length of the cylinder barrel. This arrangement could not have been considered successful, as it apparently was applied to only a limited number of units and was not carried over to the later 6-cylinder engine model. There was much experimentation with cam shapes and most probably variations of these got into production.

With the crankcase, they did not go all the way to the modern two-piece form but instead retained the one-piece construction. Assembly was effected through the ends and a detachable plate was provided on one side for access to the interior. It is clear that they regarded this ability to get at the interior of the case without major disassembly as a valuable characteristic, and later featured it in their sales literature. They were apparently willing to accept the resultant weakening of the case and continued the construction through their last engine model. The integrally cast cylinder water jackets were abandoned and the top of the crankcase was machined flat to provide a mounting deck for individual cylinders. The use of aluminum alloy was continued, and the interior of the case was provided with strengthening webs of considerable thickness, together with supporting ribs The cam shaft was supported directly in the case.

The individual cylinder design was of extreme simplicity, a single iron casting embodying everything except the water jacket. The valves seated directly on the cast-iron cylinder head and the guides and ports were all contained in an integral boss on top of the head. The exhaust valve location on the side of the engine opposite the pilot was a decided advantage over that of the 1903 design, where the exhaust was toward the pilot. A four-cornered flange near the bottom of the cylinder provided for fastening it to the crankcase, and a threaded hole in the top of the head received a vertical eyebolt which served as the rocker-arm support. The cylinder was machined all over; two flanges, one at the bottom and the other about two-thirds of the way down provided the surfaces against which the water jacket was shrunk. The jacket was an aluminum casting incorporating the necessary bosses and double shrunk on the barrel; that is, the jacket itself was shrunk on the cylinder-barrel flanges and then steel rings were shrunk on the ends of the jacket over the flanges. The jacket thickness was reduced by machining at the ends, making a semigroove into which the steel shrink rings fitted. These rings insured the maintenance of a tight joint despite the tendency of the aluminum jacket to expand away from the cast-iron barrel.

a

b

Figure 9.—4-Cylinder vertical engine: a, Magneto side; b, valve port side with intake manifold removed; c, flywheel end of engine at Carillon Park Museum, Dayton, Ohio; d, magneto side with crankcase cover removed. (Photos: a, Smithsonian A–3773; b, d, Pratt & Whitney D–15003, 15007; c, by A. L. Rockwell.)

Why the one-piece crankcase and cylinder jacket combination of the 1903 engine was abandoned for the individual cylinder construction can only be surmised. The difference in weight was probably slight, as the inherent weight advantage of the original crankcase casting was largely offset by the relatively heavy valve boxes, and the difference in the total amount of machining required, because of the separate valve boxes, cages, and attaching parts, also was probably slight. Although the crankcase had shown itself to be structurally weak, this could have been cared for by proper strengthening. The 1903 design did have some fundamental disadvantages: it required a fairly complex pattern and expensive casting, plus some difficult machining, part of which had to be very accurate in order to maintain both gas and water joints tight; and the failure of any one cylinder that affected the jacket meant a complete crankcase replacement.

It seems probable that a change was initially made mandatory by their intention to utilize the ported exhaust feature, the value of which they had proved in the experimental engine. The separate one-piece water jacket construction they had arrived at in this engine was available, but once the decision to change was made, the individual cylinder with its shrunk-on jacket had much to commend it—simplicity, cost, ease of manufacture and assembly and attachment, and serviceability. The advantages of the auxiliary, or ported, exhaust were not obtained without cost, however, as the water jacket around the barrel could not very easily be extended below the ports. Thus, even though the water was carried as high as possible on the upper end, a large portion of the barrel was left uncooled, and the lack of cooling at the lower end, in conjunction with the uncooled portion of the head, meant that only approximately half the entire cylinder surface was cooled directly.

The piston was generally the same as in the 1903 engine, except that six radial ribs were added on the under side of the head, tapering from maximum thickness at the center to nothing near the wall. They were probably incorporated as an added path for heat to flow from the center of the piston toward the outside, as their shape was not the best use of material for strength. The piston pin was locked in the piston by the usual set screw, but here no provision was made for the alternate practice of clamping the rod on the pin. This piston-pin setscrew construction had become a standard arrangement in automobile practice. The piston rings were the normal wide design of that time, with what would now be considered a low unit pressure.

Quite early in the life of this engine model the practice was initiated of incorporating shallow grooves in the surface of the more highly loaded thrust face of the piston below the piston pin to provide additional lubrication. This development apparently proceeded haphazardly. Figure 10c shows three of the pistons from an engine of low serial number—the first of this model to be delivered to the U.S. Navy—and it will be noted that one has no grooves, another has one, and the other has three. The eventual standardized arrangement provided three of these grooves, approximately 1/16 in. wide, extending halfway around the piston, and, although the depth was only a few thousandths of an inch, the amount of oil carried in them was apparently sufficient to assist in the lubrication of the face, as they were used in both the 4- and 6-cylinder engines.

Each cylinder was fastened to the crankcase by four nuts on studs driven into the aluminum case. Valves and rocker arms were similar to those of the early engines, the automatic inlet valve being retained. The continued use of the two-piece valve is not notable, even though one-piece forgings were available and in use at this time; the automobile continued for many years to use this construction. The camshaft was placed at the bottom of the engine, inside the crankcase, and the rocker arms were actuated by pushrods which were operated by hinged cam followers. The pushrod was fastened in the rocker by a pin, about which it operated, through its upper end and was positioned near the bottom by a guide in the crankcase deck. The lower end of the rod bore directly on the flat upper surface of the cam follower, and valve clearance adjustment was obtained by grinding this end. The camshaft and magneto were driven by the crankshaft through a three-member train of spur gears (see Figures 9, 10 and 11).

The built-up construction of the connecting rod was carried over from the first engine, and in the beginning apparently the same materials were used, except that the big end was babbited. Later the rod ends were changed from bronze to steel. The big end incorporated a small pointed scupper on one side for lubrication, as with the original, and this was sometimes drilled to feed a groove which carried oil to the rod bearing, but where the drilling was omitted, the only function the scupper then could perform was, as in the original engine, to throw a small amount of oil on the cylinder wall.

The crankshaft and flywheel were similar in design to those on the 1903 engine, except that the sharp corners at the top and bottom of the crank cheeks were machined off to save weight (see Figure 10f). An oil pump and a fuel pump were mounted side by side in bosses cast on the valve side of the crankcase; they were driven from the camshaft by worm gears and small shafts crossing the case.

The camshaft construction was considerably altered from the 1903 design. Although the reason is not entirely clear, one indication suggests that breakage or distortion of the shaft may have been encountered: whereas in the 1903 engine there had been no relationship between the location of

a

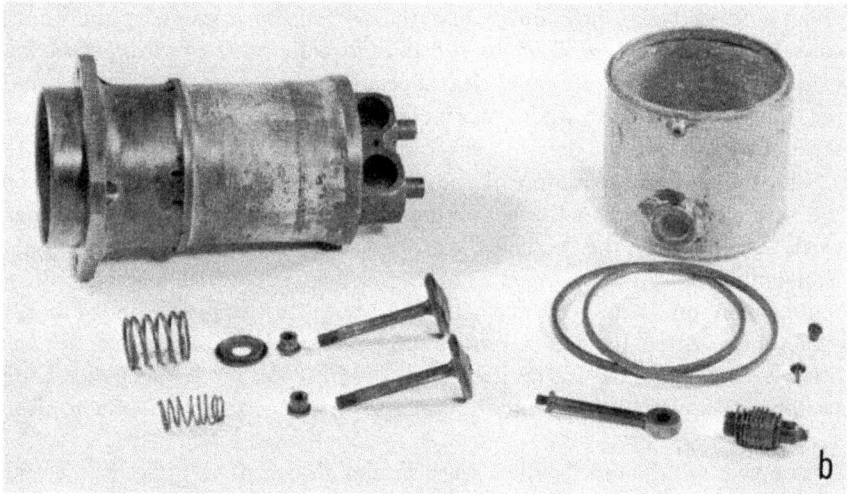

b

c

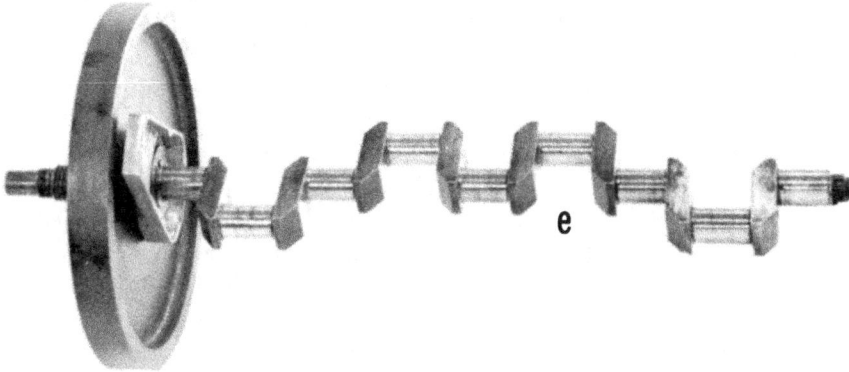

Figure 10.—4-Cylinder vertical engine: a, Cylinder assembly with valve mechanism parts; b, cylinder disassembled, and parts; c, pistons and connecting rods; d, bottom side of piston; e, crankshaft, flywheel and crankcase end closure; f, crankcase, with compression release parts. (Pratt & Whitney photos D–14996, 15001, 14998, 14994, 14999, 14989, respectively.)

the cams and the camshaft bearings, in this engine the exhaust valves were carefully positioned so that all cams were located very close to the supporting bearings in the crankcase. Also, the camshaft was solid, although it would seem that the original hollow shaft construction could have provided equal stiffness with less weight. The final decision was possibly determined by the practicality that there existed no standard tubing even approximating the size and wall thickness desired.

There still was no carburetor, a gear pump metering the fuel in the same manner as on the 1904–1905 engine. Basically, the intake charge was fed to the cylinders by a round gallery manifold running alongside the engine. This was split internally by a baffle extending almost from end to end, so that the fuel mixture entering the manifold on one side of the baffle was compelled to travel to the two ends before it could return to the inside cylinder, this feature being a copy of their 1903 general intake arrangement. Apparently various shapes and positions of entrance pipes with which to spray the fuel into the manifold were used; and the injection arrangement seems also to have been varied at different times. The fuel pump was not necessarily always used, as the engine in some of the illustrations did not incorporate one, the fuel apparently being fed by gravity, as on the original engine. Chenoweth describes an arrangement in which exhaust heat was applied to the inlet manifold to assist the fuel vaporization process, but it is believed that this was one of the many changes made in the engine during its lifetime and not necessarily a standard feature.

A water circulation pump was provided, driven directly by the crankshaft through a two-arm universal joint intended to care for any misalignment between the shaft and the pump. The water was piped to a horizontal manifold running along the cylinders just below the intake manifold, and a similar manifold on the other side of the engine collected it for delivery to the radiator. It is a little difficult to understand why it was not introduced at the bottom of the water jackets.

The crankcase was a relatively strong and well proportioned structure with three heavy strengthening ribs running from side to side, its only weakness being the one open side. A sheet-iron sump was fastened to the bottom by screws and it would appear from its design, method of attachment, and location of the engine mounting pads that this was added some time after the crankcase had been designed; but if so it was apparently retrofitted, as engines with quite low serial numbers have this part.

The ignition was by high-tension magneto and spark plug and this decision to change from the make-and-break system was undoubtedly the correct one, just as adoption of the other form originally was logical under the circumstances that existed then. The high-tension system was simpler and had now collected more service experience. The magneto was driven through the camshaft gear, and a shelf, or bracket, cast as an integral part of the case, was provided for mounting it. The spark advance control was in the magneto and, since spark timing was the only means of regulating the engine power and speed, a wide range of adjustment was provided.

The engine had the controllable compression release which had been added to the *No. 2* and *No. 3* flat engines, although mechanically it was considerably altered from the original design. Instead of the movable stop operating directly on the rocker roller to hold the exhaust valve open, it was located underneath a collar on the pushrod. This stop was hinged to the crankcase and actuated by a small rod running along and supported by the crankcase deck. Longitudinal movement of this rod in one direction would, by spring pressure on each stop, push them underneath the collars as the exhaust valves were successively opened. A reverse movement of the rod would release them (see Figure 10f). Why they retained the method of manually operating the compression release, which was the same as had been used in the 1904–1905 engine, is not quite clear. That is, the mechanism was put into operation by pulling a wire running from the pilot to a lever actuating the cam which moved the control rod. When normal valve operation was subsequently desired, the pilot was compelled to reach with his hand and operate the lever manually, whereas a second wire or push-pull mechanism would have obviated the necessity for both the awkward manual operation of the lever and the gear guard which was added to protect the pilot's hand, the lever being located close to the camshaft gear.

The 4-cylinder vertical engine was a considerable improvement over the previous designs. They had obtained a power increase of about 40 percent, with a weight decrease of 10 percent, and now had an engine whose design was almost standard form for good internal combustion engines for years to come. In fact, had they split the crankcase at the crankshaft center line and operated the inlet valves mechanically, they would have had what could be termed a truly modern design. They needed more cylinder cooling, both barrel and head, particularly the latter, and an opened-up induction system for maximum power output, but this was not what they were yet striving for. They had directly stated that they were much more interested in reliability than light weight.

This engine model was the only one of the Wright designs to be licensed and produced abroad, being manufactured in Germany by the Neue Automobil-Gesellschaft and by Bariquand et Marré in France. The latter was much more prominent and their engines were used in several early European airplanes.

The French manufacturer, without altering the basic design, made a

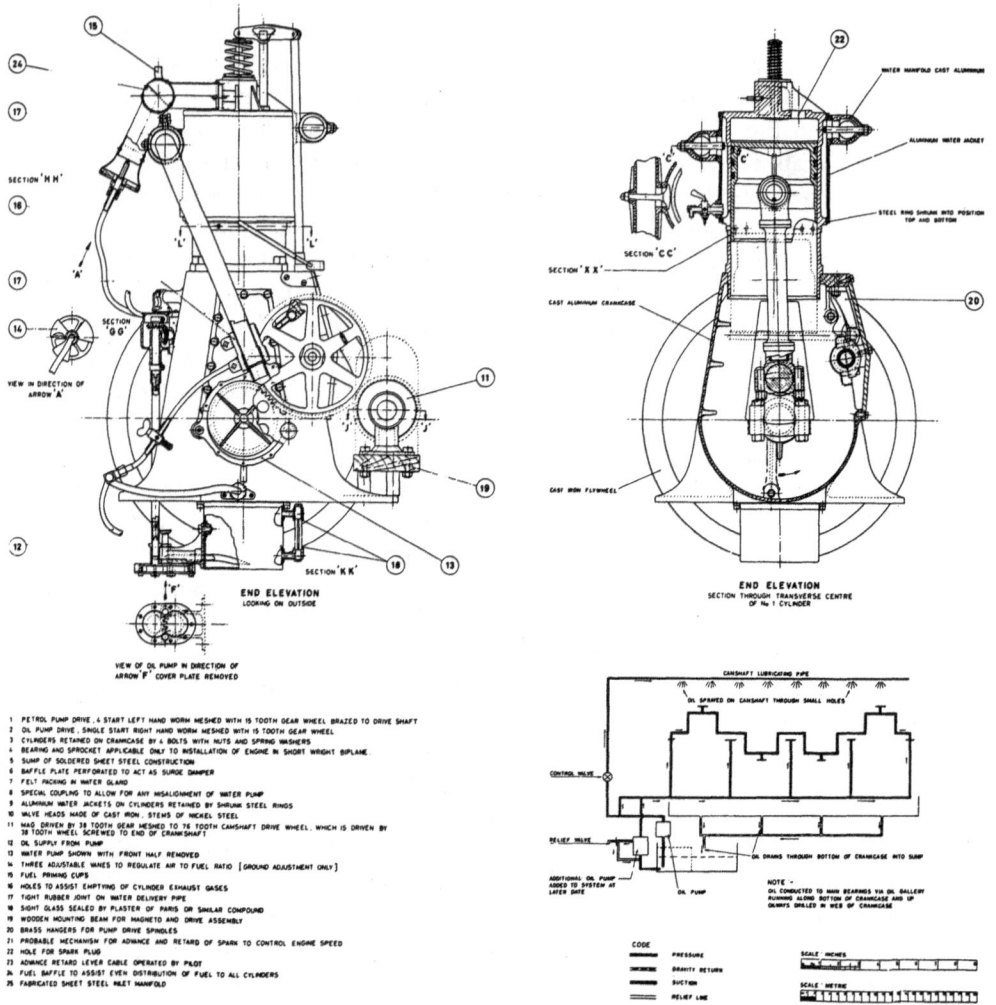

SECTION 'HH'

SECTION 'GG'

VIEW IN DIRECTION OF
ARROW 'A'

SECTION 'KK'

END ELEVATION
LOOKING ON OUTSIDE

VIEW OF OIL PUMP IN DIRECTION OF
ARROW 'P' COVER PLATE REMOVED

SECTION 'XX'

SECTION 'CC'

WATER MANIFOLD CAST ALUMINIUM

ALUMINIUM WATER JACKET

STEEL RING SHRUNK INTO POSITION
TOP AND BOTTOM

CAST ALUMINIUM CRANKCASE

CAST IRON FLYWHEEL

END ELEVATION
SECTION THROUGH TRANSVERSE CENTRE
OF No 1 CYLINDER

CAMSHAFT LUBRICATING PIPE

OIL SPRAYED ON CAMSHAFT THROUGH SMALL HOLES

CONTROL VALVE

RELIEF VALVE

ADDITIONAL OIL PUMP
ADDED TO SYSTEM AT
LATER DATE

OIL PUMP

OIL DRAWN THROUGH BOTTOM OF CRANKCASE INTO SUMP

NOTE -
OIL CONDUCTED TO MAIN BEARINGS VIA OIL GALLERY
RUNNING ALONG BOTTOM OF CRANKCASE AND UP
DRILLINGS DRILLED IN WEB OF CRANKCASE

CODE
PRESSURE
GRAVITY RETURN
SUCTION
RELIEF LINE

SCALE INCHES

SCALE METRE

1 PETROL PUMP DRIVE. 4 START LEFT HAND WORM MESHED WITH 15 TOOTH GEAR WHEEL BRAZED TO DRIVE SHAFT
2 OIL PUMP DRIVE. SINGLE START RIGHT HAND WORM MESHED WITH 15 TOOTH GEAR WHEEL
3 CYLINDERS RETAINED ON CRANKCASE BY 6 BOLTS WITH NUTS AND SPRING WASHERS
4 BEARING AND SPROCKET APPLICABLE ONLY TO INSTALLATION OF ENGINE IN SHORT WRIGHT BIPLANE.
5 SUMP OF SOLDERED SHEET STEEL CONSTRUCTION
6 BAFFLE PLATE PERFORATED TO ACT AS SURGE DAMPER
7 FELT PACKING IN WATER GLAND
8 SPECIAL COUPLING TO ALLOW FOR ANY MISALIGNMENT OF WATER PUMP
9 ALUMINIUM WATER JACKETS ON CYLINDERS RETAINED BY SHRUNK STEEL RINGS
10 VALVE HEADS MADE OF CAST IRON. STEMS OF NICKEL STEEL
11 MAG DRIVEN BY 38 TOOTH GEAR MESHED TO 76 TOOTH CAMSHAFT DRIVE WHEEL, WHICH IS DRIVEN BY
   38 TOOTH WHEEL SCREWED TO END OF CRANKSHAFT
12 OIL SUPPLY FROM PUMP
13 WATER PUMP SHOWN WITH FRONT HALF REMOVED
14 THREE ADJUSTABLE VANES TO REGULATE AIR TO FUEL RATIO [GROUND ADJUSTMENT ONLY]
15 FUEL PRIMING CUPS
16 HOLES TO ASSIST EMPTYING OF CYLINDER EXHAUST GASES
17 TIGHT RUBBER JOINT ON WATER DELIVERY PIPE
18 SIGHT GLASS SEALED BY PLASTER OF PARIS OR SIMILAR COMPOUND
19 WOODEN MOUNTING BEAM FOR MAGNETO AND DRIVE ASSEMBLY
20 BRASS HANGERS FOR PUMP DRIVE SPINDLES
21 PROBABLE MECHANISM FOR ADVANCE AND RETARD OF SPARK TO CONTROL ENGINE SPEED
22 HOLE FOR SPARK PLUG
23 ADVANCE RETARD LEVER CABLE OPERATED BY PILOT
24 FUEL BAFFLE TO ASSIST EVEN DISTRIBUTION OF FUEL TO ALL CYLINDERS
25 FABRICATED SHEET STEEL INLET MANIFOLD

Figure 11.—4-Cylinder vertical engine assembly, Bariquand et Marré version.
(Drawing courtesy Bristol Siddeley Engines, Ltd.)

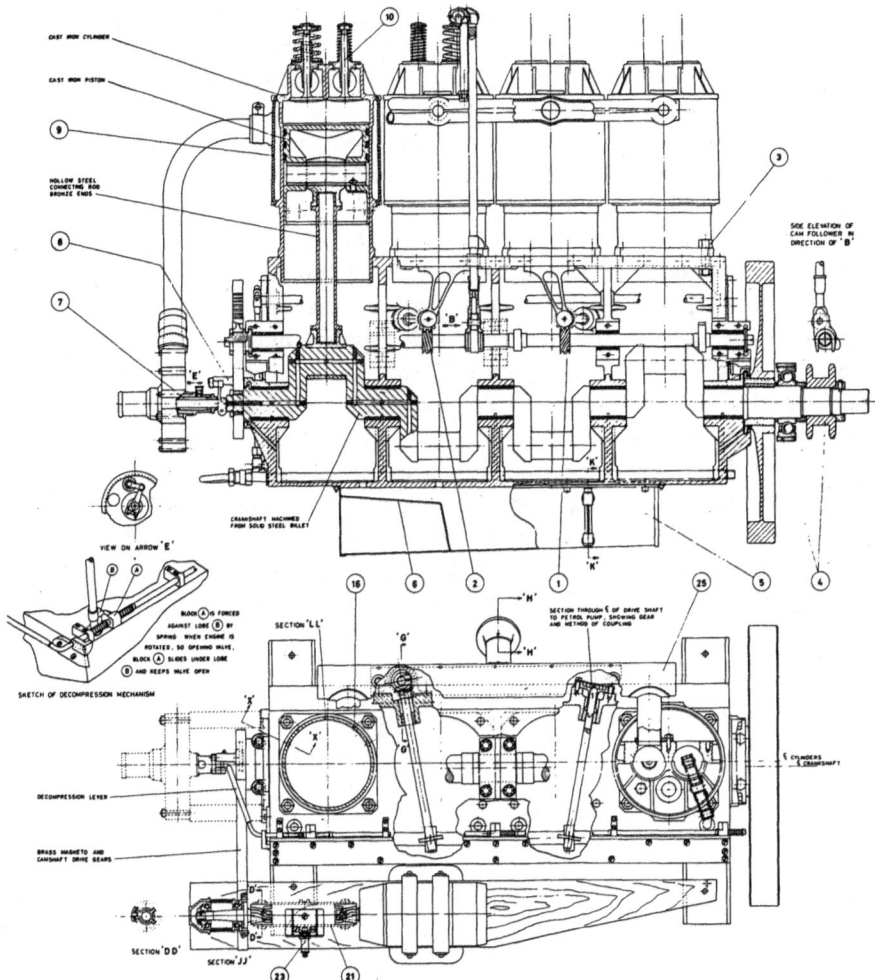

THE WRIGHT BROTHERS AERO ENGINE

PARTICULARS OF ENGINE	
BORE	112 mm
STROKE	111 mm
SWEPT VOLUME	4372 cc
COMPRESSION RATIO	4 185
RATED POWER	30 HP at 1300 RPM
WEIGHT	217 92 LBS

MADE BY BARIQUAND AND MARRÉ OF PARIS AND INSTALLED IN ONE OF THE SIX "SHORT WRIGHT BIPLANES" BUILT AT EASTCHURCH IN 1909 - 1910 BY SHORT BROTHERS LTD UNDER THE FIRST PRODUCTION CONTRACT EVER PLACED FOR AIRCRAFT

DRAWING PREPARED FROM THE PARTS OF AN ENGINE HELD BY SHORT BROTHERS AND HARLAND LTD BELFAST

45

number of changes of detail which seem to have greatly annoyed Wilbur Wright, although some of them could probably be listed as improvements, based on several features of later standard design. One consisted of an alteration in the position of the fuel and oil pumps, the latter being lowered to the level of the sump. The crankcase was drilled to provide forced-feed lubrication to the connecting rod big end and crankshaft main bearings. Strengthening ribs were added to the pistons running from the upper side of the pin bosses to the piston wall, and the crankcase studs holding down the cylinders were replaced with bolts having their heads inside the case. The hinged cam follower was omitted and the pushrod bore directly on the cam through a roller in its end. The magneto was moved toward the rear of the engine a considerable distance and an ignition timing control device was introduced between it and its driving gear. Instead of the magneto being mounted directly on the special bracket integral with the crankcase, a wooden board running from front to rear of the engine was used and this was fastened to the two engine support pads, the magneto bracket being omitted entirely.

Despite his criticism of the French motor and the quality of its manufacture, Wilbur was compelled to install one in his own exhibition airplane during his early French demonstrations at Le Mans after rod failure had broken his spare crankcase, and much of his subsequent demonstration flying was made with the French product.

The Eight-Cylinder Racing Engine

By 1909 regular and special air meets and races were being held and various competitions for trophies conducted. Among these the Gordon Bennett Cup Race for many years was considered a major event. For the 1910 competition it was decided to enter a Wright machine and, since this was a race with speed the sole objective, the available 4-cylinder engine, even in a version pushed to its maximum output, was deemed too small. They built for it a special 8-cylinder unit in a 90°V form. They were thus resorting to one of their 1904 concepts—modifying and enlarging a version known and proved in use—as the proper method of most quickly increasing output. Unfortunately again, there are essentially no detailed drawings available, so that the design cannot be studied.[16]

Only one engine is historically recorded as having been built, although in view of the Wrights' record of foresight and preparation it is almost certain that at least one spare unit, assembled or in parts, was provided. In any case, the airplane—it was called the *Baby Grand Racer*—and engine were wrecked just before the race, and no physical parts were retained, so that the sole descriptions come from external photographs, memory, and heresay. McFarland thinks that possibly Orville Wright, particularly, was somewhat discomfitted over the accident that eliminated the machine, as he had previously flown it quite successfully at a speed substantially higher than that of the ultimate winner, and he wanted to get it out of sight and mind as quickly as possible. The Air Force Museum at Wright Field, Dayton, Ohio, has an incomplete set of drawings of a 90°V, 8-cylinder Wright engine, but it is quite obvious from the basic design and individual features, as well as from at least one date on the drawings, that this conception is of a considerably later vintage than that of the *Baby Grand Racer*.

The racing engine was in essence a combination of two of the standard 4s on a redesigned crankcase utilizing as many of the 4-cylinder engine parts as possible. The rods were reported to have been placed side by side, and the regular 4-cylinder crankshaft, with alterations to accommodate

---

[16]A drawing of the camshaft is held by The Franklin Institute.

the rods, was utilized. A single cam operated all the exhaust valves. It was compact and light, its only fundamental disadvantage being the inherent unbalance of the 90°V-8. The arrangement provided a much higher powered unit in the cheapest and quickest manner, and one that could be expected to operate satisfactorily with the least development.

a

b

The Six-Cylinder Vertical Engines

Shortly after the construction of the 8-cylinder engine the Wrights were again faced with the ever-recurrent problem of providing a higher powered standard production engine for their airplanes, which were now being produced in some numbers. By this time, 1911, there had been a relatively tremendous growth in both flying and automotive use of the internal combustion engine and as a result many kinds and sizes had been produced and utilized, so that numerous choices were presented to them. But if they

Figure 12.—Original 6-cylinder engine: a, Push-rod side; b, valve-port side; c, crankcase with sump removed. (Photos: Smithsonian A–3773A, 45598; Pratt & Whitney D–15015, respectively.)

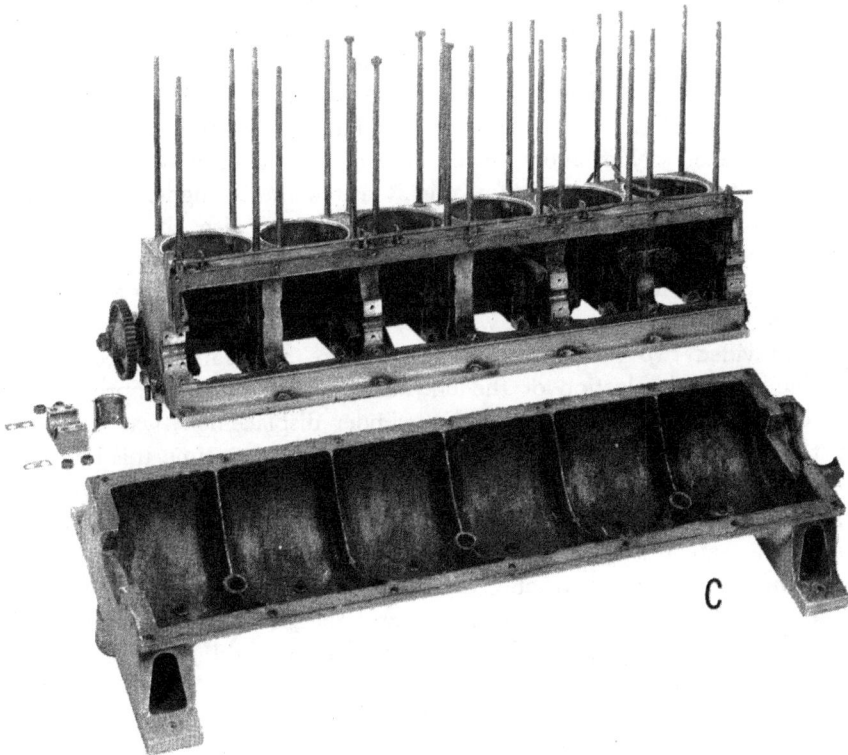

were both to make use of their past experience and retain the simplicity they had always striven for, the more practical possibilities narrowed down to three: they could increase the cylinder size in the 4-cylinder combination, or they could go either to 6 or 8 cylinders in the approximate size they had previously used.

The 4-in. cylinder in combination with a 5-in. stroke would provide in four cylinders about the displacement they wanted. Strokes of 6 in. were not uncommon and cylinders of 6-in. bore had been very successfully utilized in high-output automobile racing engines many years before this, so there was seemingly no reason to doubt that the 5-in. cylinder could be made to operate satisfactorily, but it is not difficult to imagine the Wrights' thoughts concerning the roughness of an engine with cylinders of this diameter. The question of the grade of available fuel may possibly have entered into their decision to some extent, but it seems far more likely that roughness, their perennial concern, was the predominant reason for not staying with the more simple 4-cylinder form (as we have seen, roughness to them meant the effect of the cylinder explosion forces). Actually, of course, they never went larger than a 4⅜-in. cylinder bore, and later aircraft engine experience would seem generally to confirm their judgment, for with the piston engine it has always been much more difficult to make the larger bores operate satisfactorily at any given specific output.

While the 90°V, 8-cylinder arrangement would have enabled them to utilize a great number of the 4-cylinder-engine parts, it would have given them a somewhat larger engine than was their apparent desire, unless they reduced the cylinder size. And while they had had some limited experience in building and operating this kind of engine, and twice had chosen it when seeking more power, both of these choices were greatly influenced by the desire to obtain quickly an engine of higher power. It is also possible that something in their experience with the V-8 moved them away from it; the unbalanced shaking force inherent in the arrangement may well have become evident to them. What probably also helped them to their final conclusion was the fundamental consideration that the V-8 provided two extra cylinders which were not really needed.

The eventual selection of the 6-cylinder was a slight compromise. In order to get the desired output the cylinder displacement was increased, but this was done by lengthening the stroke—the first time this had been altered since the original design. The increase (from 4 to 4½ in.) was only ½ in., and the bore, the more important influence on fuel performance, was kept the same. Overall, the choice was quite logical. They were utilizing the in-line construction upon which almost all of their now considerable experience had been based, and the sizes of and requirements for parts also conformed to this experience. They could, in fact, use many of the same parts. The natural balance of the 6-cylinder arrangement gave them a very smooth engine, and had they stiffened the shaft and counter-weighted the cranks, they would have produced the smoothest engine that could have been built at that time.

In the literature are two references to a Wright 6-cylinder engine constructed around the cylinders of the vertical 4. One of these is in Angle's *Airplane Engine Encyclopedia*, published in 1921, and the other is in *Aerosphere 1939*, published in 1940. The wording of the latter is essentially identical with that of the former; it seems a reasonable conclusion that it is a copy. Although it is possible that such an engine was built at some time, just as the 8-cylinder racing engine was cobbled up out of parts from the 4-cylinder vertical, no other record, no engines, and no illustrations have been found. It is thus quite certain that no significant quantity was ever manufactured or utilized.

The crankcase was considerably changed from that of the vertical 4, and was now in two pieces, with the split on the crankshaft center line. However, the shaft was not supported by the lower half of the case, as eventually became standard practice, but by bearing caps bolted to the ends of the upper case and, in between, to heavy ribs running across the upper case between the cylinders. The lower half of the case thus received none of the dynamic or explosion loads, and, serving only to support the engine and to provide for its mounting, was lightly ribbed. In it were incorporated integral-boss standpipe oil drains which discharged into a bolted-on sump. The upper half of the case was again left open on one side, giving the desired access to the interior, and, additionally, the design was altered to provide a method of camshaft assembly that was much simpler than that of the vertical 4 (see p. 42).

The cylinder was also greatly altered from that of the vertical 4. It was made in three parts, a piece of seamless steel tubing being shrunk on a cast-iron barrel to form the water jacket, with a cast-iron cylinder head shrunk on the upper end of the barrel. This construction compelled the use of long studs running from the cylinder head to the case for fastening down the cylinder (see Figures 12a-c). For the first time the cylinder heads were water-cooled, cored passages being provided, and more barrel surface was jacketed than previously, although a considerable area at the bottom was still left uncooled, obviously by direct intent, as the ported exhaust arrangement was no longer employed.

Also for the first time one-piece forged valves were used, but just when these were incorporated is not certain and, surprisingly, they were applied to the inlet only, the exhaust valve being continued in the previous two-piece screwed and riveted construction. The reasoning behind this is not evident. If a satisfactory two-piece exhaust valve had finally been developed it

51

would be logical to carry it over to the new design; but exhaust valves normally being much more troublesome, it would seem that a good exhaust valve would make an even better inlet valve and, in the quantities utilized, the two-piece design should have been much cheaper. In the original 6-cylinder engine the inlet valves operated automatically as in all previous models, but at the time of a later extensive redesign (1913) this was changed to mechanical actuation, and the succeeding engines incorporated this feature. All the valve-actuating mechanism was similar to that of the vertical 4, and the engine had the usual compression-release mechanism, the detail design being carried over directly from the 4-cylinder.

Design of the piston followed their previous practice, with wide rings above the pin and shallow grooves below the pin on the thrust face, and with the pin fastened in the piston by a set screw. The piston had four ribs underneath the head (see Figure 13b) radiating from the center and with the two over the pin bosses incorporating strengthening webs running down and joining the bosses. The piston length was reduced by 1 in., thus giving a much less clumsy appearance and, with other minor alterations, a weight saving of 40 percent (see Figures 13b and c). The rods were for the first time made of I-section forgings, a major departure, machined on the sides and hand finished at the ends, with a babbit lining in the big end, the piston pin bearing remaining steel on steel.

At least two different general carburetion and induction systems were utilized, possibly three. One, and most probably the original, consisted of a duplicate of the injection pump of the 4-cylinder fitted to a manifold which ran the length of the engine, with three takeoffs, each of which then split into two, one for each cylinder. Of this arrangement they tried at least two variations involving changes in the location and method of injecting the fuel into the manifold; and there seems to have been an intermediate manifold arrangement, using fuel-pump injection at the middle of the straight side, or gallery, manifold, which was fed additional air at both ends through short auxiliary inlet pipes. This would indicate that with the original arrangement, the end cylinders were receiving too rich a mixture, when the fuel in the manifold was not properly vaporized. Although the exhaust was on the same side of the engine as the inlet system, no attempt was made to heat the incoming charge at any point in its travel. An entirely different system adopted at the time of the complete redesign in 1913 consisted of two float-feed Zenith carburetors each feeding a conventional

Figure 13.—Original 6-cylinder engine: a, Cylinder assembly and valve parts; b, bottom side of piston; c, piston, piston pin and connecting rod; d, valve mechanism; e, crankshaft and flywheel. (Pratt & Whitney photos D–15012, 15017, 15013, 15018, respectively.)

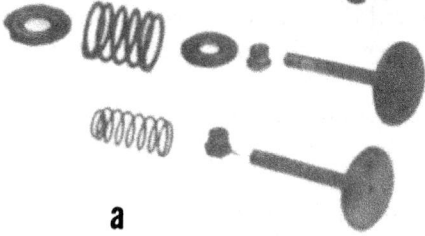

a

b

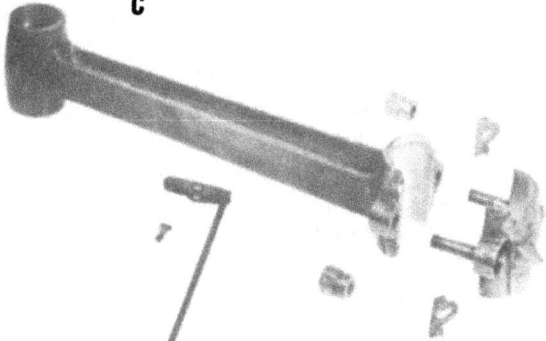

c

d

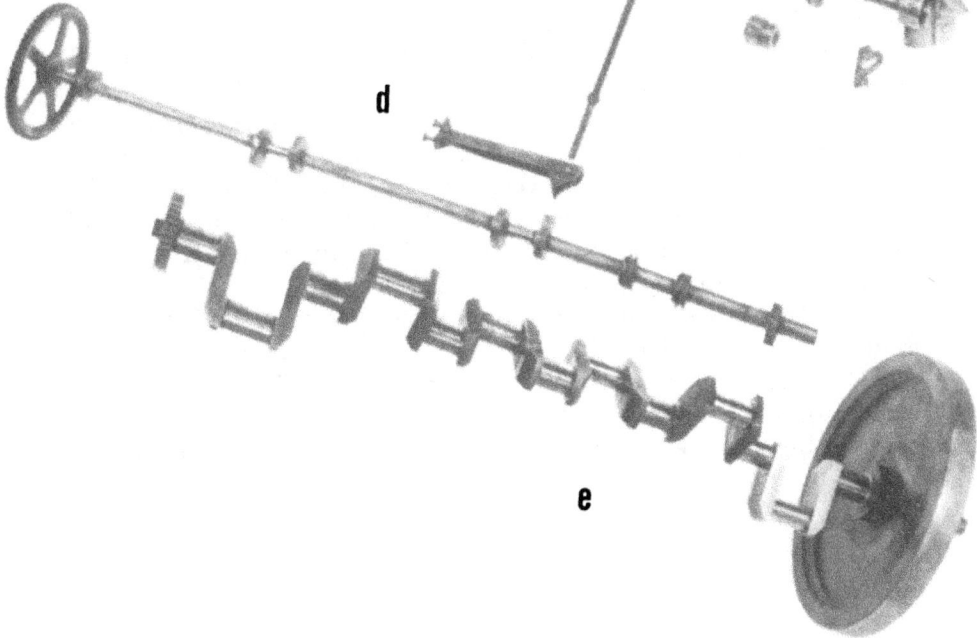

e

three-outlet manifold. This carburetor was one of the first of the plain-tube type, that is, with the airflow through a straight venturi without any spring-loaded or auxiliary air valves, and was the simplest that could be devised. When properly fitted to the engine, it gave a quite good approximation of the correct fuel and air mixture ratio over the speed-load running range, although it is considerably more than doubtful that this was maintained at altitude, as is stated in one of the best descriptions of the engine published at the time the carburetors were applied.

The compression ratio of this engine was lowered by almost 20 percent from that of the vertical 4. This, in combination with the low bore-to-stroke ratio, the unheated charge, and the later mechanically operated inlet valve, indicates that the Wrights were now attempting for the first time to secure from an engine something approaching the maximum output of which it was capable.

As the engine originally came out, it continued to utilize only one spark plug in each cylinder. The high-tension magneto had a wide range of spark advance adjustment, which again provided the only control of the engine when equipped with the original fuel pump injection.

The location of the valves and pushrods was similar to that in the 4, so that the cams were immediately adjacent to the camshaft bearings, which were carried in the crankcase ends and in the heavy webs. The camshaft was gear-driven and the cam shape was similar to that of the last 4s, with a quite rapid opening and closing and a long dwell, leaving the valve opening accelerations and seating velocities still quite high.

The crankshaft was a continuation of their basic design of rather light construction, particularly in the webs. The cheeks were even thinner (by 1/4 in.) than those of the 4 although the width was increased by 1/8 in. (see Figure 13e). For the first time they went to a forging, the rough contour type of the time, and utilized a chrome-nickel alloy steel.

Lubrication was by means of the usual gear pump, and the piston and rod bearings continued to be splash-fed. The rod big-end bearing carried a small sharp undrilled boss at the point where, on the other engines, had been located scuppers whose purpose was apparently still to throw lubricating oil on the cylinder wall carrying the more highly loaded side of the piston. The rod big-end bearing was lubricated by a hole on the top of the big-end boss catching some of the crankcase splash, which was then carried to the bearing by a groove.

When the 6-cylinder engine was completely redesigned in 1913 this led to the introduction in late fall of that year of a new model called the 6–60, the 60 designating the rating in horsepower. There is little in the Wright records to show why such a radical revision was thought necessary, but the general history of the period gives a rather clear indication. The competition had caught up to the Wrights in powerplants. Other engines were being installed in Wright airplanes, and Navy log books show these other engines being used interchangeably with those of the Wrights.

Most of the descriptions of the new model published at the time it was introduced concentrate on the addition of the two carburetors and the mechanical operation of the inlet valves, but these were only two of many major changes. The cylinder was completely revised, the intake being moved to the camshaft side of the engine from its position adjacent to the exhaust, so that the two ports were now on opposite sides of the cylinder. By proper positioning of the rocker-arm supports and choice of their length and angles, all valves were made operable from a single camshaft. The shrunk-on steel water jacket cylinder was retained, but the water connections were repositioned so that the water entered at the bottom and came out at the top of the cylinder. Over the life of the 6-cylinder engine several different valve types were used but the published specifications for the model 6–60 called for "cast iron heads"—the old two-piece construction. The piston pins were case hardened and ground and the crankshaft pins and journals were heat treated and ground.

The fuel and oil pumps were removed from the side of the crankcase and a different ignition system was applied, although still of the high-tension spark-plug type which by this time had become general practice on all so-called high-speed internal-combustion engines. A second threaded spark-plug hole was provided in the cylinder head and despite its more common use for other purposes, it is evident that the intention was to provide two-plug ignition. It is doubtful that at the specific output of this engine any power difference would be found between one- and two-plug operation, so that the objective was clearly to provide a reserve unit in case of plug failure. However, it was also used for the installation of a priming cock for starting and because of the prevalence of single-wire ignition systems on existing and illustrated engines, it seems to have been used mostly in this manner, even though dual-ignition systems later became an unvarying standard for aircraft engines.

Viewed externally, the only part of the engine that appears the same as the original 6 is the small lower portion of the crankcase; but what is more visually striking is the beauty of the new lines and extreme cleanness of the exterior design (see Figures 14 and 15). Many of their individual parts had shown the beauty of the sparse design of pure utility but it was now in evidence in the whole. Despite the proven practical value of their other models, this is the only one that can be called a good-looking engine, instantly appealing to the aesthetic sense, even though the vertical 4 is not an ugly engine. The appearance of their final effort, in a field they were originally reluctant to enter and concerning which they always deprecated the results of their own work, was a thing of which a technically trained professional engine designer could be proud.

The 6–60 was continued in production and development until it became the 6–70, and indications are that it eventually approached an output of 80 horsepower.

Figure 14.—6-Cylinder 6–60 and 6–70 engine, right rear intake side. (Pratt & Whitney photo.)

Figure 15.—6-Cylinder 6–70 engine, incorporating flexible flywheel drive, exhaust side. (Smithsonian photo A–54381.)

Minor Design Details and
Performance of the Wright Engines

In the Wright brothers' various models were many minor design items which altogether required a great deal of consideration, but which did not materially affect overall engine performance. The results generally could all be classed as good practice; however, one of these utilized in the 4-cylinder vertical engine was rather unorthodox and consisted of offsetting the cylinders with relation to the crankshaft. This arrangement, which can be seen in the drawing (Figure 11) was apparently an attempt to reduce the maximum side load on the piston during the power stroke, but since the peak gas loading usually occurs at about 10 to 15 percent of the power stroke, this probably did not have much effect, and it was not carried over to the 6-cylinder design.

All engine bearings were of the plain sleeve type and, except for the bronze and steel bearings in the connecting rod, were of babbit. The advantages of babbit for bearings were discovered very early in the development of the mechanical arts, and apparently the Wrights never encountered a bearing loading sufficiently high to cause a structural breakdown in this relatively weak material.

Valve openings show no variation through the successive production engines, although the Wrights most probably experimented with different amounts. The 1903 engine and the vertical 4- and 6-cylinder all had lifts of 5/16 in., but the valve-seat angles varied somewhat; the records show included angles of 110° to 90°—not a large difference.

The valve-operating mechanism was the same from the first vertical 4 onward. The high side thrust caused by the cam shape required for the very rapid valve opening they chose was, no doubt, the reason for the use of the hinged cam follower, and since the same general cam design was used in their last engine, the 6-cylinder, the same method of operation which had apparently proved very serviceable was continued. How satisfactory was the considerably simpler substitute used in the Bariquand et Marré version of the 4-cylinder engine is not known. Possibly it was one of the alterations in the Wrights' design that Wilbur Wright objected to, although in principle it more closely conforms to the later fairly standard combination valve tappet and roller construction: The available drawings do indicate, however, that the cam of the Bariquand et Marré engine was also altered to give a considerably less abrupt valve opening than the Wright design, so that there was less side thrust. For the Wright 6-cylinder engine their 4-cylinder cam was slightly altered to provide a rounding off near the top of the lobe, thus providing some reduction in the velocity before maximum opening was reached. All their cam designs indicate a somewhat greater fear of the effect of seating velocities than of opening accelerations.

Since the range of cylinder diameters utilized did not vary greatly, the valve sizes were correspondingly fairly uniform. The diameter of the valves for the original 4-in.-bore cylinder was 2 in., while that for the 4⅜-in. bore used in the 6-cylinder engine was actually slightly smaller, 1⅞ in. Possibly the Wrights clung too long to the automatic inlet valve, although it did serve them well; but possibly, as has been previously noted, there were valid reasons for continuing its use despite the inherently low volumetric efficiency this entailed.

The inherent weakness in the joints of the three-piece connecting rod has been pointed out, but aside from this, the design was excellent, for all the materials and manufacturing methods required were readily available, and structurally it was very sound. Tubular rods were still in use in aircraft engines in the 1920s.

The Wrights had a surprisingly thorough grasp of the metallurgy of the time, and their choice of materials could hardly have been improved upon. Generally they relied upon the more simple and commonly used metals even though more sophisticated and technically better alloys and combinations were available.[17] Case hardening was in widespread use in this period but their only utilization of it was in some parts of the drive chains purchased completely assembled and in the piston pins of their last engine. The treatment of the crankshafts of all their engines except the final 6-cylinder was typical of their uncomplicated procedure: the particular material was chosen on the basis of many years of experience with it, hardening was a very simple process, and the expedient of carrying this to a

---

[17] Baker states that the first crankshaft was made from a slab of armor plate and if this is correct the alloy was a rather complex one of approximately .30–.35 carbon, .30–.80 manganese, .10 silicon, .04 phosphorus, .02 sulphur, 3.25–3.50 nickel, 0.00–1.90 chromium; however, all the rest of the evidence, including Orville Wright's statement to Dr. Gough, would seem to show that it was made of what was called tool steel (approximately 1.0 carbon).

point just below the non-machinable range gave them bearing surfaces that were sufficiently hard, yet at the same time it eliminated the possibility —present in a heat-treating operation—of warping the finished piece.

In the entire 1903 engine only five basic materials—excepting those in the purchased "magneto" and the platinum facing on the ignition-system firing points—were used: steel, cast iron, aluminum, phosphor bronze, and babbit. The steels were all plain carbon types with the exception of the sheet manifold, which contained manganese, and no doubt this was used because the sheet available came in a standard alloy of the time.

Overall, the Wright engines performed well, and in every case met or exceeded the existing requirements. Even though aircraft engines then were simpler than they became later and the design-development time much shorter, their performance stands as remarkable. As a result, the Wrights never lacked for a suitable powerplant despite the rapid growth in airplane size and performance, and the continual demand for increased power and endurance.

Few service records dating from before 1911, when the military services started keeping log books, have been found. Some of those for the period toward the end of their active era have been preserved, but for that momentous period spanning the first few years when the Wrights had the only engines in actual continuous flight operation, there seems to be essentially nothing—perhaps because there were no standard development methods or routines to follow, no requirements to be met with respect to pre-flight demonstrations or the keeping of service records. Beginning in 1904, however, and continuing as long as they were actively in business, they apparently had in progress work on one or more developmental or experimental engines. This policy, in combination with the basic simplicity of design of these engines, accounted in large measure for their ability to conduct both demonstrations and routine flying essentially whenever they chose.

Time between engine overhauls obviously varied. In mid 1906 an engine was "rebuilt after running about 12 hours." This is comparatively quite a good performance, particularly when it is remembered that essentially all the "running" was at full power output. It was considerably after 1920 before the Liberty engine was redesigned and developed to the stage where it was capable of operating 100 hours between overhauls, even though it was being used at cruising, or less than full, power for most of this time.

The Wrights of course met with troubles and failures, but it is difficult, from the limited information available, to evaluate these and judge their relative severity. Lubrication seems to have been a rather constant problem, particularly in the early years. Although some bearing lubrication troubles were encountered from time to time, this was not of major proportions, and they never had to resort to force-feed lubrication of the main or rod big-end bearings. The piston and cylinder-barrel bearing surfaces seem to have given them the most trouble by far, and examination of almost any used early Wright engine will usually show one or more pistons with evidence of scuffing in varying degrees, and this is also apparent in the photographs in the record. This is a little difficult to understand inasmuch as most of the time they had the very favorable operating condition of cast iron on cast iron. Many references to piston seizure or incipient seizure, indicated by a loss of power, occur, and this trouble may have been aggravated by the very small piston clearances utilized. Why these small clearances were continued is also not readily explainable, except that with no combination of true oil-scraper rings, which was the basic reason why the final form of aviation piston engine was able to reach its unbelievably low oil consumptions, their large and rather weak compression rings were probably not doing an adequate job of oil control, and they were attempting to overcome this with a quite tight piston fit.[18] In any event, they did encounter scuffing or seizing pistons and cylinder over-oiling at the same time. As late as 4 May 1908 in the Wright *Papers* there appears the notation: "The only important change has been in the oiling. The engine now feeds entirely by splash . . . ."

Their troubles tended to concentrate in the cylinder-piston combination, as has been true of almost all piston engines. References to broken clyinders are frequent. These were quite obviously cylinder barrels, as replacement was common, and this again is not readily explainable. The material itself, according to Orville Wright, had a very high tensile strength, and in the 1903 engine more than ample material was provided, as the barrel all the way down to well below the attachment to the case was 7/32 in. thick. The exact location of the point of failure was never recorded, but in its design are many square corners serving as points of stress concentration. Also, of course, no method was then available for determining a faulty casting, except by visual observation of imperfections on the surface, and this was probably the more common cause. It is interesting, however, that the engine finally assembled in 1928 for installation in the 1903 airplane sent to England has a cracked cylinder barrel, the crack originating at a

---

[18] Their intended piston ring tension is not known. Measurements of samples from the 4- and 6-cylinder vertical engines vary greatly, ranging from less than ½ lb per sq in. to almost 1¼ lb. The validity of these data is very questionable as they apply to parts with unknown length of service and amount of wear. It seems quite certain, however, that even when new the unit tension figure with their wide rings was only a small fraction of that of the modern aircraft piston engine.

sharp corner in the slot provided at the bottom of the barrel for screwing it in place.

Valve failures were also a continuing problem, and Chenoweth reports that a large proportion of the operating time of the 1904–1906 development engine was concentrated on attempts to remedy this trouble. None of their cams, including those of the 6-cylinder engine, evidence any attempt to effect a major reduction in seating velocities. United States Navy log books of 1912 and 1913 record many instances of inlet valves "broken at the weld," indicating that some of the earlier 6-cylinder engines were fitted with valves of welded construction.

For the engineer particularly, the fascination of the Wrights' engine story lies in its delineation of the essentially perfect engineering achievement by the classic definition of engineering—to utilize the available art and science to accomplish the desired end with a minimum expenditure of time, energy, and material. Light weight and operability were the guiding considerations; these could be obtained only through constant striving for the utmost simplicity. Always modest, the Wrights seem to have been even more so in connection with their engine accomplishments. Although the analogy is somewhat inexact, the situation is reminiscent of the truism often heard in the aircraft propulsion business—few people know the name of Paul Revere's horse. Yet, as McFarland has pointed out, "The engine was in fact far from their meanest achievement." With hardly any experience in this field and only a meagerly equipped machine shop, they designed and assembled an internal combustion engine that exceeded the specifications they had laid down as necessary for flight and had it operating in a period of about two months elapsed time. The basic form they evolved during this unequalled performance carried them through two years of such successful evolutionary flight development that their flying progressed from a hop to mastery of the art. And the overall record of their powerplants shows them to have been remarkably reliable in view of the state of the internal combustion engine at that time.

Appendix

Characteristics of the Wright Flight Engines

	1903 First flight engine [a]	1904–1905 Experi- mental flights	1908–1911 Demonstra- tions and service	1911–1915 service
Cyl./Form	4/flat	4/flat	4/vertical	6/vertical
Bore and stroke (in.)	4×4	4-1/8×4	4-3/8×4	4-3/8×4-1/2
Displacement (cu. in.)	201	214	240	406
Horsepower	8.25–16	15–21	28–42	50–75
RPM	670–1200	1070–1360	1325–1500	1400–1560
MEP	49–53	52–57	70–87	70–94
Weight (lb)	140–180	160–170	160–180	265–300

[a] Concurrently with the Wrights' first engine work, Manly was developing the engine for the Langley Aerodrome, and a comparison of the Wrights' engine development with that of Manly is immediately suggested, but no meaningful comparison of the two efforts can be drawn. Beyond the objective of producing a power unit to accomplish human flight and the fact that all three individuals were superb mechanics, the two efforts had nothing in common. The Wrights' goal was an operable and reasonably lightweight unit to be obtained quickly and cheaply. Manly's task was to obtain what was for the time an inordinately light engine and, although the originally specified power was considerably greater than that of the Wrights, it was still reasonable even though Manly himself apparently increased it on the assumption that Langley would need more power than he thought. The cost and time required were very much greater than the Wrights expended. He ended up with an engine of extraordinary performance for its time, containing many features utilized in much later important service engines. His weight per horsepower was not improved upon for many years. The Wrights' engine proved its practicability in actual service. The Manly engine never had this opportunity but its successful ground tests indicated an equal potential in this respect. A description of the Langley-Manly engine and the history of its development is contained in *Smithsonian Annals of Flight* number 6, "Langley's Aero Engine of 1903," by Robert B. Meyer (xi + 193 pages, 44 figures; Smithsonian Institution Press, 1971)

It is not possible to state the exact quantities of each engine that the Wrights produced up to the time that their factory ceased operation in 1915. Chenoweth gives an estimate, based on the recollection of their test foreman, of 100 vertical 4s and 50 6s. My estimate (see page 2) places the total of all engines at close to 200. Original Wright-built engines of all four of these basic designs are in existence, although they are rather widely scattered. The Smithsonian's National Air and Space Museum has examples of them all, including, of course, the unique first-flight engine. Their condition varies, but many are operable, or could easily be made so. Among the best are the first-flight engine and the last vertical 6, at the Smithsonian, the first vertical 6, at the United States Air Force Museum, and the vertical 4, at the Carillon Park Museum.

The Wrights were constantly experimenting and altering, and this in connection with the lack of complete records makes it almost impossible to state with any certainty specific performances of individual engines at given times. Weights sometimes included accessories and at others did not. Often they were of the complete powerplant unit, including radiator and water and fuel, with no clarification. In the table, performance is given in ranges which are thought to be the most representative of those actually utilized. Occasionally performances were attained even beyond the ranges given. For example, the 4x4-in. flat development engine eventually demonstrated 25 hp at an MEP of approximately 65 psi.

One important figure—the horsepower actually utilized during the first flight—is quite accurately known. In 1904 the 1904–1905 flight engine, after having been calibrated by their prony-brake test-fan method, was used to turn the 1903 flight propellers, and Orville Wright calculated this power to be 12.05 bhp by comparing the calibrated engine results with those obtained with the flight engine at Kitty Hawk when tested under similar conditions. However, since the tests were conducted in still air with the engine stationary, this did not exactly represent the flight condition. No doubt the rotational speed of the engine and propellers increased somewhat with the forward velocity of the airplane so that unless the power-rpm curve of the engine was flat, the actual horsepower utilized was probably a small amount greater than Orville's figures. The lowest power figure shown for this engine is that of its first operation.

No fuel consumption figures are given, primarily because no comprehensive data have been found. This is most probably because in the early flight years, when the Wrights were so meticulously measuring and recording technical information on the important factors affecting their work, the flights were of such short duration that fuel economy was of very minor importance. After success had been achieved, they ceased to keep detailed records on very much except their first interest—the flying machine itself—and when the time of longer flights arrived, the fuel consumption that resulted from their best engine design efforts was simply accepted. The range obtained became mostly a matter of aerodynamic design and weight carried. Orville Wright quotes an early figure of brake thermal efficiency for the 1903 engine that gives a specific fuel consumption of .580 lb of fuel per bhp/hr based on an estimate of the heating value of the fuel they had. This seems low, considering the compression ratio and probable leakage past their rather weak piston rings, but it is possible. In an undated entry, presumably in 1905, Orville Wright's notebook covered fuel consumption in terms of miles of flight; one of the stated assumptions in the entry is, "One horsepower consumes .60 pounds per horsepower hour"—still quite good for the existing conditions. Published figures for the 6–60 engine centered around .67 lb/hp hr for combined fuel and oil consumption.

The Wright Shop Engine

Despite the fact that the Wright shop engine was not a flight unit, it is interesting both because it was a well designed stationary powerplant with several exceedingly ingenious features, and because its complete success was doubtless a major factor in the Wrights' decision to design and build their own first flight engine. Put in service in their small shop in the fall of 1901, it was utilized in the construction of engine and airframe parts during the vital years from 1902 through 1908 and, in addition, it provided the sole means of determining the power output of all of their early flight engines. By means of a prony brake, its power output was carefully measured and from this the amount of power required for it to turn certain fans or test clubs was determined. These were then fitted to the flight engines and the power developed calculated from the speed at which the engines under test would turn the calibrated clubs. Although a somewhat complex method of using power per explosion of the shop engine was made necessary by the basic governor control of the engine, the final figures calculated by means of the propeller cube law seem to have been surprisingly accurate.[19] Restored under the personal direction of Charles Taylor, it is in the Henry Ford Museum in Dearborn, Michigan, together with the shop machinery it operated.

The engine was a single cylinder, 4-stroke-cycle "hot-tube" ignition type. The cylinder, of cast iron quite finely and completely finned for its

---

[19] *The Papers of Wilbur and Orville Wright,* volume 2, Appendix.

Figure 16.—Shop engine, 1901, showing governor and exhaust
valve cam.   (Photo courtesy R. V. Kerley.)

day, was air-cooled, or rather, air-radiated, as there was no forced circulation of air over it, the atmosphere surrounding the engine simply soaking up the dissipated heat. Although this was possibly a desirable adjunct in winter, inside the small shop in Dayton, the temperature there in summer must have been quite high at times. The operating fuel was city illuminating gas, which was also utilized to heat, by means of a burner, the ignition tube. This part was of copper, with one completely closed end positioned directly in the burner flame; the other end was open and connected the interior of the tube to the combustion chamber. The inlet valve was of the usual automatic type while the exhaust valve was mechanically operated. The fuel gas flow was controlled by a separate valve mechanically connected to the inlet valve so that the opening of the inlet valve also opened the gas valve, and gas and air were carried into the cylinder together.

The engine was of normal stationary powerplant design, having a heavy base and two heavy flywheels, one on each side of the crank. These were necessary to ensure reasonably uniform rotational speed, as, in addition to having only one cylinder, the governing was of the hit-and-miss type. It had a 6x7-in. bore and stroke and would develop slightly over 3 hp at what was apparently its normal operating speed of 447 rpm, which gives an MEP of 27 psi.

The engine is noteworthy not only for its very successful operation but also because it incorporated two quite ingenious features. One was the speed-governing mechanism. As in the usual hit-and-miss operation, the engine speed was maintained at a constant value, the output then being determined by the number of power strokes necessary to accomplish this. The governor proper was a cylindrical weight free to slide along its axis on a shaft fastened longitudinally to a spoke of one of the flywheels. A spring forced it toward the center of the wheel, while centrifugal force pulled it toward the rim against the spring pressure. After each opening of the valve the exhaust-valve actuating lever was automatically locked in the valve-open position by a spring-loaded pawl, or catch. The lever had attached to it a small side extension, or bar, which, when properly forced, would release the catch and free the actuating lever. This bar was so positioned as to be contacted by the governor weight when the engine speed was of the desired value or lower, thus maintaining regular valve operation; but an excessive speed would move the governor weight toward the rim and the exhaust valve would then be held in the open position during the inlet stroke, so no cylinder charge would be ingested. Since the ignition was not mechanically timed, the firing of the charge was dependent only on the compression of the inlet charge in the cylinder, so it made no difference whether the governor caused the engine to cease firing for an odd or even number of revolutions, even though the engine was operating on a 4-stroke cycle at all times.

The exhaust valve operating cam was even more ingenious. To obtain operation on a 4-stroke cycle and still avoid the addition of a half-speed camshaft, a cam traveling at crankshaft speed was made to operate the exhaust valve every other revolution (see Figure 17). It consisted of a very slim quarter-moon outline fastened to a disc on the crankshaft by a single bearing bolt through its middle which served as the pivot about which it moved. Just enough clearance was provided between the inside of the quarter-moon and the crankshaft to allow the passage of the cam-follower roller. The quarter-moon, statically balanced and free to move about its pivot, basically had two positions. In one the leading edge was touching the shaft (Figure 17b), so that when the cam came to the cam follower, the follower was forced to go over the top of the cam, thus opening the exhaust valve. When the cam pivot point had passed the roller, the pressure of the exhaust valve spring forced the following edge of the cam

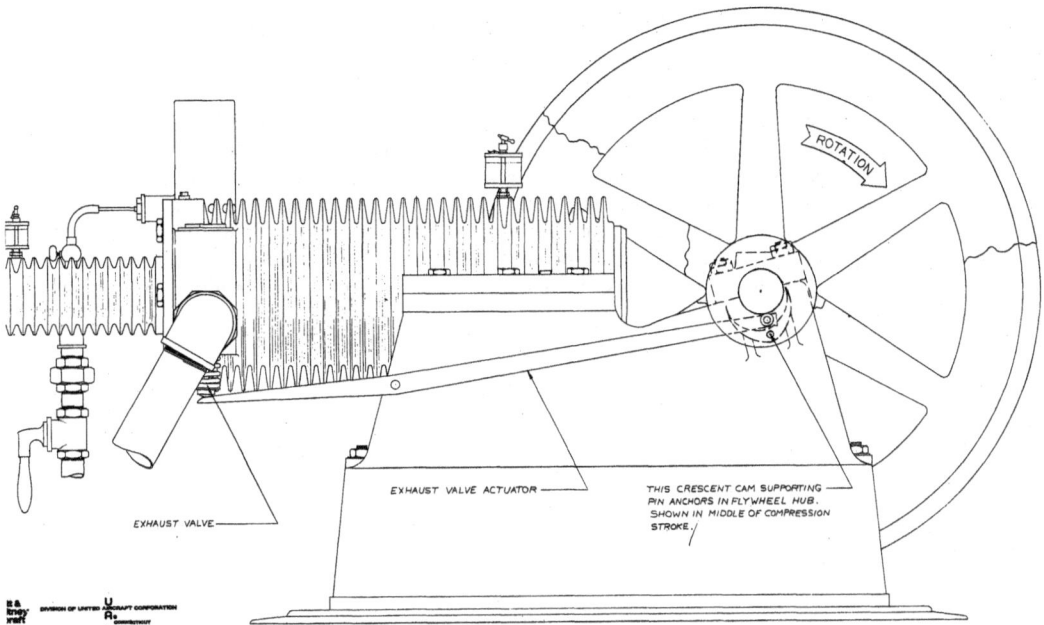

ROTATION

EXHAUST VALVE ACTUATOR

THIS CRESCENT CAM SUPPORTING
PIN ANCHORS IN FLYWHEEL HUB.
SHOWN IN MIDDLE OF COMPRESSION
STROKE.

EXHAUST VALVE

DR8768

a   *b*   *c*   *d*

END OF COMPRESSION STROKE   START OF EXHAUST STROKE   END OF EXHAUST STROKE   START OF COMPRESSION STROKE

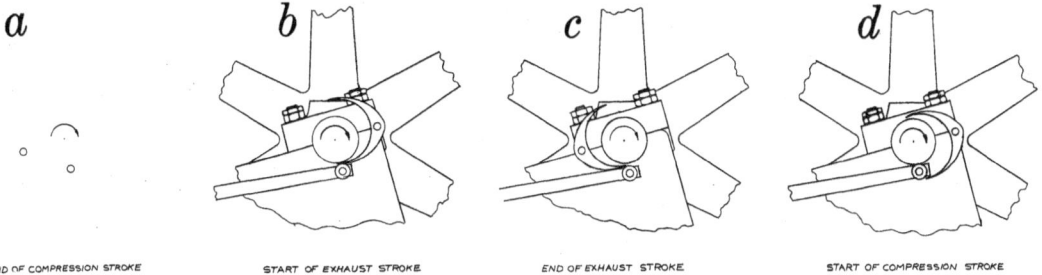

Figure 17.—Shop engine, 1901, showing operation of exhaust
valve cam.   (Pratt & Whitney drawing.)

into contact with the shaft and this movement, which separated the leading edge of the cam from the shaft, provided sufficient space between it
and the shaft for the roller to enter (Figure 17c). Thus, when the leading
edge of the cam next reached the roller, the roller, being held against the
crankshaft by the valve spring pressure (Figure 17d), entered the space
between the cam and the shaft and there was no actuation of the valve.
In exiting from the space, it raised the trailing edge of the cam, forcing the
leading edge against the shaft (Figure 17a) so that at the next meeting a
normal valve opening would take place. The cam was maintained by fric-

tion alone in the position in which it was set by the roller, but since the amount of this could be adjusted to any value, it could be easily maintained sufficient to offset the small centrifugal force tending to put the cam in a neutral position.[20]

[20] The Wrights apparently never applied for an engine patent of any kind. This no doubt grew out of their attitude of regarding the engine as an accessory and deprecating their work in this field. A reasonably complete patent search indicates that this particular cam device has never been patented, although a much more complex arrangement accomplishing the same purpose was patented in 1900, and a patent application on a cam-actuating mechanism substantially identical to that of the Wrights and intended for use in a golf practice apparatus is pending at the present time.

Bibliography

ANGLE, GLENN D. Wright. Pages 521–523 in *Airplane Engine Encyclopedia, an Alphabetically Arranged Compilation of All Available Data on the World's Airplane Engines.* Dayton, Ohio: The Otterbein Press, 1921.

BAKER, MAX P. The Wright Brothers as Aeronautical Engineers. *Annual Report of . . . the Smithsonian Institution . . . for the Year Ended June 30, 1950,* pages 209–223, 4 figures, 9 plates.

BEAUMOUNT, WILLIAM WORBY. *Motor Vehicles and Motors: Their Design, Construction, and Working by Steam, Oil, and Electricity. 2 volumes.* Philadelphia: J. B. Lippincott, 1901–1902.

CHENOWETH, OPIE. Power Plants Built by the Wright Brothers. *S.A.E. Quarterly Transactions* (January 1951), 5:14–17.

FOREST, FERNAND. *Les Bateaux automobiles.* Paris: H. Dunod et E. Pinat, Éditeurs, 1906.

GOUGH, DR. H. J. Materials of Aircraft Construction. *Journal of the Royal Aeronautical Society* (November 1938), 42:922–1032. Illustrated.

KELLY, FRED C. *Miracle at Kitty Hawk; the Letters of Wilbur and Orville Wright.* New York: Farrar, Straus and Young, 1951.

—————————. *The Wright Brothers, a Biography Authorized by Orville Wright.* New York: Harcourt, Brace & Co., 1943.

KENNEDY, RANKIN. *Flying Machines: Practice and Design. Their Principles, Construction and Working.* 158 pages. London: Technical Publishing Co., Ltd., 1909.

LAWRANCE, CHARLES L. *The Development of the Aeroplane Engine in the United States.* Pages 409–429 in International Civil Aeronautics Conference, Washington, D.C., 12–14 December 1928, Papers Submitted by the Delegates for Consideration by the Conference. Washington: Government Printing Office, 1928.

McFARLAND, MARVIN W. *The Papers of Wilbur and Orville Wright.* 2 volumes. New York: McGraw Hill Book Co., 1953.

RENSTROM, ARTHUR G. Wilbur and Orville Wright: A Bibliography Commemorating the Hundredth Anniversary of the Birth of Wilbur Wright, April 16, 1867. Washington, D.C.: The Library of Congress [Government Printing Office], 1968. Contains 2055 entries.

The 6-Cylinder 60-Horsepower Wright Motor. *Aeronautics* (November 1913), 13(5):177–179.

Wright Brothers. Pages 829–830 in *Aerosphere 1939, Including World's Aircraft Engines, with Aircraft Directory*, Glenn D. Angle, editor. New York: Aircraft Publishers, 1940.

Index

☆ U.S. GOVERNMENT PRINTING OFFICE: 1971—397–764